版权法导论

汉 英 对 照

The ABC of Copyright

联合国教科文组织 / 著

张雨泽◎译 郭寿康◎审校

知识产权出版社

内容提要

本书以浅显的语言概述版权的历史和现在，除介绍传统的版权之外，还介绍了伴随着新技术发展而产生的新型权利，全面反映了版权法的最新发展，具有崭新的内容。

原著由联合国教科文组织编写，本版以中英文对照的方式出版，以期对愿意了解版权法的社会公众和有志攻读版权法英文原著的青年学子有所帮助。

责任编辑：刘　睿　　**责任校对**：韩秀天
装帧设计：张冀书装　　**责任出版**：卢运霞

图书在版编目（CIP）数据

版权法导论/联合国教科文组织著．—北京：知识产权出版社，2009.1

书名原文：The ABC of Copyright

ISBN 978-7-80247-198-6

Ⅰ．版…　Ⅱ．联…　Ⅲ．版权-著作权法-研究　Ⅳ．D913.04

中国版本图书馆 CIP 数据核字（2008）第 198266 号

版权法导论

联合国教科文组织　著

张雨泽　译　郭寿康　审校

出版发行：知识产权出版社

社　址：	北京市海淀区马甸南村 1 号	邮　编：	100088
网　址：	http：//www.ipph.cn	邮　箱：	bjb@cnipr.com
发行电话：	010-82000860 转 8101	传　真：	010-82000889
责编电话：	010-82000860 转 8113	责编邮箱：	liurui@cnipr.com
印　刷：	北京富生印刷厂	经　销：	新华书店及相关销售网点
开　本：	880mm×1230mm　1/32	印　张：	6.25
版　次：	2009 年 1 月第 1 版	印　次：	2009 年 1 月第 1 次印刷
字　数：	161 千字	定　价：	20.00 元

ISBN 978-7-80247-198-6/D·751（2234）

本书的出版，得到了联合国教科文组织的支持和资助，谨表谢意。

序　言

版权是知识产权的一个重要组成部分。知识产权在我国现代社会中越来越具有重要的作用。胡锦涛主席指出："当今世界，国家的核心竞争越来越表现为对智力资源和智慧成果的培育、配置、调控能力，表现为对知识产权的拥有、运用能力"；"加强我国知识产权制度建设，大力提高知识产权创造管理、保护、运用能力"；"要充分发挥知识产权在增强国家经济科技实力和国际竞争力、维护国家利益和经济安全方面的重要作用，为我国进入创新型国家行列提供强有力的支撑"。

《版权法导论》的翻译和出版，是为了给广大公众提供一本学习、了解版权法的优秀读物。本书由联合国教科文组织编写，于20多年前初版发行，并曾译成中文出版。时至今日，随着科学技术的重大进步和社会经济的迅速发展，版权法也产生了重大变化，国际上缔结并实施了TRIPs协定、WIPO版权条约以及WIPO表演和录音制品条约。本书新版全面反映了版权法的最新发展，具有崭新的内容。从而，中国人民大学联合国教科文组织版权与邻接权教席受联合国教科文组织的委托，将新版译成中文，并以中英文对照的方式出版。希望能够对愿意了解、学习版权法的广大公众和有志于攻读版权法外文原著的青年学子有所帮助。

本书的特点，一是浅显易懂，尽可能避免晦涩艰深的术语而使用较为平直的语言，使从未接触过版权的读者也能明了相关内容；二是篇幅虽然短小，但内容丰富，基本囊括了版权的历史和现在，除介绍传统的版权之外，还介绍了伴随着新技术发展而产生的新型权利。

限于译校者的水平，译文不妥之处，诚恳希望读者不吝指正。

郭寿康

2008年10月9日

CONTENT

目　录

Copyright—Past and Present

Introduction

Today we live in a world of instant global communications. Everyone is familiar with the technological developments that have come with dazzling rapidity. New techniques for recording and transmitting texts, sound or visual images have proliferated. Digital technology has created prodigious capacities to store, disseminate and retrieve knowledge.

These technologies are providing unprecedented possibilities for communication between people as well as for the development of cultural industries and exploitation of works all over the world. At the same time, the possibility of piracy of protected works has increased dramatically. It is thus not surprising that in many countries, as well as in the international arena, copyright laws and international standards are being regularly revised to meet the challenges of new technologies.

Copyright law plays now more than ever an important role in the modern world. This introductory chapter aims at providing an understanding of this complex legal domain by taking also a look at its underlying principles and the way copyright laws have evolved over the centuries in response to technological developments and society's needs.

版权——过去和现在

引言

今天，我们生活在一个全球瞬时交流的世界。每个人对技术令人眩目的迅猛发展已经习以为常。对文件、声音或者可视图像进行录制和传播的新技术激增。数字技术为知识的存储、传播和检索创造出巨大的潜力。

这些技术为人们的交流和文化产业的发展以及全球范围内作品的使用提供了空前的可能性。同时，对受保护作品的盗版的可能性也显著增加。因此，在许多国家，包括在国际社会内，对版权法和国际标准的定期修订以应对新技术的挑战也就不令人感到意外了。

在当今世界，版权法发挥的作用较以往任何时候都重要。引言这一章的目的是通过观察版权法的基本原则和其几个世纪以来为适应技术进步和社会需求而逐渐形成的过程，从而使人对这一复杂的法律领域有所理解。

Copyright
• Central role in culture and communication
• Intrinsically linked to technological advances
• Challenged by rampant piracy in many countries

What is copyright?

Copyright is a branch of law that grants authors (writers, musicians, artists and other creators) protection over their works. Such protection consists in providing authors with ownership or property rights (or exploitation rights), which take into account their material interests. Under copyright, authors are entitled to protection against unauthorised use of their works as well as possibly to a share in any earnings from its use by the public.

But copyright laws may also provide protection for another set of interests, of a more personal nature, which are commonly called the "moral rights" of authors. These rights allow the author to claim authorship in her work as well as respect for its integrity.

The protection of moral and material interests resulting from any scientific, literary or artistic production is also recognised as a human right under the Universal Declaration of Human Rights (1948) and the International Covenant on Economic, Social and Cultural Rights (1966)

Copyright is part of the law of intellectual property (IP), which protects other subject matter as well, such as trade marks, patents, designs, plant seed varieties, trade secrets, integrated circuits, and topographies. All topics that come under the heading of intellectual

版权
• 在文化交流中的中心作用
• 与技术进步的内在联系
• 在许多国家面临猖獗盗版的挑战

什么是版权？

版权是法律的一个分支，对作者（作家、音乐家、艺术家和其他创作者）的作品给予保护。版权保护包括授予作者们以所有权或者财产权（或利用权），这些权利都涉及作者的物质利益。依版权，作者有权得到保护以制止未经其授权而使用其作品，以及享有公众使用其作品而获得的收益。

而且，版权法还可以对另外一些更具有人身性质的利益提供保护，这通常被称做作者的"精神权利"。此类权利使作者可以享有作品的署名权和完整权。

对于科学研究，文学和艺术创作而产生的精神利益和物质利益进行保护也是《世界人权宣言》（1948）和《经济、社会和文化权利国际公约》（1966）所承认的人权。

版权是知识产权法的一部分，知识产权法还保护其他客体，诸如商标、专利、外观设计、植物品种、商业秘密、集成电路和拓扑图。所有这些被知识产权所保护的项目都有共同的一个事实，即被保护者为获得她所受保护的成果而投入了大量的智力劳动。

property have in common the fact that the protected person has displayed an amount of her intellect in achieving the results for which she is protected.

Yet copyright laws do not only aim at establishing individual rights for the benefit of authors, they also take into account the needs of users and of society at large for access to knowledge and information. In order to maintain a fair balance between the conflicting interests, copyright protection is subject to a number of exceptions and limitations. The interplay between exclusive rights, on the one hand, and exceptions and limitations to these rights, on the other, forms the legal framework within which creativity and communication may develop.

The Essence of Copyright
• Right of ownership in creative works
• Protection against unauthorised uses
• Limitations for the benefit of society at large

How is copyright protection justified?

There are two main justifications for the legal protection provided by copyright. The first argumentation is linked to economic considerations, the second line of thought stems from theories referring to natural law. Practically all copyright laws have taken into account elements from these two lines of argument, although different countries may give varying emphasis to each of them.

From an economic point of view, the grant of an exclusive right ensures for the author an economic reward for the exploitation of the

然而，版权法不仅仅是为了建立针对作者个人权利的保护，还要考虑作品使用者的需要和社会自由获得知识和信息的需要。为了合理平衡两者之间的利益冲突，版权保护要有一些例外和限制。专有权与其限制和例外交互影响，构成了一个法律框架，在此框架下，创造和传播才得以发展。

版权的本质
• 创造性作品的所有权
• 保护作者制止未经授权的使用
• 为整个社会利益而设的限制

如何论证版权的保护

有关版权所提供的法律保护主要有两项理由。第一项论证与经济利益考虑相关联，第二项论证源于与自然法相关的理论。在实践中，所有的版权法都将这两项论证元素考虑在内，虽然各国对二者强调的重点有所不同。

从经济观点来看，授予作者以专有权可以保证作者对一定期限内使用其作品获得经济回报，从而鼓励创作。

work for a certain period and hence constitutes an incentive for creativity.

According to justifications based on natural law, on the other hand, each person has a natural right of property to the products of her labour. It is argued that this must also apply in the case of intellectual creations.

The economic argument has been particularly prevalent in countries which are part of the Anglo-American world, while the doctrine of natural law has had greater influence on the European continent and in countries of Roman law tradition. Accordingly, we may distinguish two major traditions in copyright law, the Anglo-American, or common law copyright system, and the continental European, or civil law *author's right* system. As this terminology might suggest, the former tends to emphasise the protection of the *work*, while the latter is rather centred on the personality of the work's *creator*. The distinction becomes particularly relevant with respect to such questions as moral rights or a legal entity's eligibility as author.

The Rationale behind Copyright
• Exclusive rights as economic reward and stimulus for creativity
• Natural/personal right in the results of intellectual work
• Distinction between Anglo-American and Continental tradition

Where lies the origin of copyright?

The origin of copyright has been linked to the European invention of printing (the Gutenberg press) in the fifteenth century. History shows however that prior to that event some form of protection existed

另一方面，按照建立在自然法基础上的理论，每个人都对通过自己劳动创造出的产品自然享有财产权利，但这一点在应用于智力创造的情况是有争议的。

经济论证特别在英美法系国家中相当流行，而自然法理论在欧洲大陆和罗马法传统国家中则有巨大影响。从而，我们可以区分在版权法上的两大传统，即英美法或普通法下的版权体系和欧洲大陆或民法法系下的“作者”权体系。版权这一术语倾向于强调对作品的保护，而作者权则更看重于作品创作者的人格，这种区分对于诸如作者精神权利或法人能否成为作者等问题是有很大意义的。

版权背后的理论基础
• 经济回报的独占权及对创作的鼓励
• 智力作品产生的自然/人身权利
• 英美法系和大陆法系传统的区分

版权的起源

版权的起源是于15世纪欧洲印刷术（谷登堡印刷机）的发明相联系的。然而历史表明，远在这一事件出现之前就存在对创作成果的某些保护形式。例如，远在古希腊和罗马时代，剽窃就

in relation to creative output. For example, already in ancient Greece and Rome, plagiarism was widely condemned as dishonourable. Moreover, ethnographers argue also that, stretching back to the earliest historical times, examples existed where some rights were recognized in respect of works and trademarks among various peoples. It took however several centuries before the pecuniary and moral interests of authors were formally recognised in the legal systems.

The invention of printing in Europe marks a decisive date as it has transformed the conditions for dissemination of printed works in an unprecedented way. Secular rulers and the clergy, both in England and on the European continent, quickly recognised the printing press as a new powerful social influence and began to grant privileges to certain printers in order to control the distribution of printed works. From the late fifteenth to the early eighteenth century, the history of printing was marked by the issuance of various royal decrees and statutes, which may be considered as the precursors of today's copyright laws.

The Origins of Copyright
• From the earliest days some forms of protection
• 15th century in Europe: Invention of the printing press
• Printing privileges precursors of modern copyright laws

When did the first copyright laws come into existence?

In 17th century England, under the influence of the philosopher *John Locke* and others, ideas of individualism emerged and the parliamentary

被认为是不诚实而广受谴责的。再者，人种史学家也论证追溯到更久远的历史时期，那时就有对各民族之间的作品和商标承认具有某些权利的例证。但是，作者的经济利益和精神利益最终在法律体系中得到正式认可却经历了几个世纪。

欧洲印刷术的发明是一个划时代的标志，它以史无前例的方式改变了印刷品传播的环境。无论在英格兰还是欧洲大陆，世俗统治者和神职人员都很快认识到印刷机具有强大的新的社会影响力，并开始授予一些印刷商特权以控制印刷品的发行。从15世纪后期到18世纪早期，印刷业的历史带有各皇室命令和制定法的色彩，这也许可看做是今天版权法的先驱。

版权的起源
• 源于早期某些保护形式
• 15世纪的欧洲：印刷术的发明
• 现代版权法的先驱是早期的印刷特权

第一批版权法是何时出现的?

17世纪的英格兰，在哲学家约翰·洛克和其他一些人的影响下，个人主义思潮涌现，代议制度取代了专制君主制度。在此

system replaced the absolute monarchy. In this period of changes, booksellers and printers started to push for some kind of copyright protection, referring to the theory of intellectual property. On 10 April 1710 a law hitherto known as The Statute of Queen Anne was passed. It was the first law on copyright in the modern sense of the term since it recognised for the first time the existence of an individual right to authors to be protected, albeit only with respect to their books.

Further important steps in the evolution of copyright were taken in France at the end of the eighteenth century. Inspired by revolutionary ideals, the decrees of 1791 and 1793 instituted in particular the concept of literary property. At the same time, the notion of public domain was introduced, and thus two fundamental principles in modern copyright were established. The French example was soon followed by other countries and by the middle of the nineteenth century, many States, including some in Latin America, had already enacted national copyright laws.

The First Copyright Laws
• 1710: Statute of Queen Anne (England)
• 1791 and 1793: Revolutionary decrees (France)
• By the middle of the 19th century: followed by many countries

How has the contemporary copyright system developed?

The modern system of copyright and related rights is substantially driven by international agreements. Already at the end of the nineteenth century, a considerable number of countries had recognised

历史转折时期，书商和印刷者开始力促对版权的某种保护，并涉及了知识产权理论。1710 年 4 月 10 日，闻名至今的《安娜女王法》获得通过。这是第一部具有现代意义的版权法，它第一次明确了作者个人权利应受保护，尽管只是对他们著作的保护。

版权演化中更重要的阶段发生在 18 世纪末的法国。在革命理想的鼓舞下，1791 年和 1793 年的法令特别规定了文学财产的概念。与此同时，公共领域的观念被引入，从而建立了现代版权的两项基本原则。法国模式很快被其他国家所效仿，在 19 世纪中叶，许多国家，包括一些拉美国家都颁布了国家版权法。

第一批版权法
• 1710 年：《安娜女王法》（英格兰）
• 1791 年和 1793 年：大革命时期法令（法国）
• 19 世纪中叶：许多国家效仿法国

当代版权体系是如何发展的?

现代版权和相关权利体系主要是由国际协议推动的。在 19 世纪末期，众多的国家已经认识到对作品的保护不能局限于国境以内。因而，一系列双边条约得以签署，尤其是在欧洲

that the protection for works should not stop at a country's borders. A number of bilateral agreements were thus signed, in particular among European countries.

The first multilateral international treaty on the protection of copyright, the Berne Convention for the Protection of Literary and Artistic Works, was signed in 1886, at the initiative of ALAI (Association Littéraire et Artistique Internationale). Since then a number of revisions have taken place and other treaties have come into existence, for instance the 1952 Universal Copyright Convention administered by UNESCO, the 1994 TRIPs Agreement (which constitutes an Annex to the Marrakech Agreement establishing the World Trade Organization) and most recently the WIPO Treaties of 1996 (WCT and WPPT), which aim at providing adequate protection for works in the new digital environment.

The increase in cross-border trade and technological developments have been the reasons which triggered recent international developments. The current challenges to copyright presented by the information society require evermore a global approach. Care should be displayed by legislators so as to ensure that copyright protection will be adequately provided for and enforced in the new digital environment, while at the same time lawful access to works will not be impeded. Thus the information society could fulfil its cultural and economic potentials.

The Modern Copyright System
• Marked by the conclusion of international agreements
• Cross-border trade and technological advances as motor
• Information society requires further global cooperation

国家之间。

第一部保护版权的多边国际条约，即《保护文学艺术作品伯尔尼公约》是在国际文学艺术协会（ALAI）的倡议下于1886年签署的，此后进行了一系列的修订并且其他条约也开始出现，例如，1952年联合国教科文组织管理下的《世界版权公约》，1994年的TRIPs协定（该协定构成了《创建世贸组织马拉喀什协定》的附件）以及最新的1996年《世界知识产权组织条约》（WCT和WPPT），WCT和WPPT的目的是在新的数字环境下对作品提供充分保护。

跨境贸易的增长和技术的发展已经成为近来国际发展的动因，而信息社会对版权提出的新一轮的挑战，要求今天采取全球的视角。所以，立法者们须尽心确保在新的数字环境中，版权保护能够得到充分的规定和执行，同时合法获得作品的渠道也不能被阻塞，从而，信息社会的经济和文化潜力方能得以发掘实现。

现代版权体系

- 以缔结国际协定为标志
- 跨境贸易和技术进步是动力
- 信息社会需要深入的国际合作

The Scope of Copyright Protection

Introduction

International conventions as well as most national laws mention that copyright law extends to "works of a literary, scientific or artistic nature". But what constitutes a work? Generally speaking, the work has to be more than a mere idea and has to be original. These two basic notions of copyright law will be explored in more details below. In recent years there has been a trend towards extending the scope of protected works, both on the international and national levels. Recent additions concern in particular computer programs and databases. Last but not least, a rather controversial case is the protection of traditional cultural expressions of local communities (often referred to as "folklore"), which are also to be dealt with below.

The Scope of Copyright Protection
• Copyright protects "works of a literary, scientific or artistic nature"
• Works must be original and more than mere ideas
• Trend towards extension of scope in recent years

What is the distinction between a protected work and a mere idea?

The distinction between protected works and ideas lies at the very

版权保护的范围

引言

国际公约以及大多数国家的法律都规定版权法范围及于“文学、科学和艺术作品”。但构成一部作品的要素是什么？通常而言，作品不仅仅是思想，而且还必须有原创性。版权法的这两个基本概念将在下文中详细地进行探讨。近年来，出现一种潮流，即在国际和国内两个层面上扩展受保护作品的范围。最近又特别增加了计算机程序和数据库。最后（但不是不重要）的一点，是地区社会传统文化表达（通常称之为“民间文学艺术”）的保护。对这个问题颇有争议，下面将进行分析。

版权保护的范围
• 版权保护“文学、科学和艺术作品”
• 作品必须是原创性的，不仅仅是单纯的思想
• 近年来扩展版权保护范围的潮流

受保护的作品和单纯的思想之间的区别是什么？

受保护作品和单纯思想之间的区别是版权法的核心问题。一

heart of copyright law. The protection of a given work applies to the *expressions* of ideas that are contained therein. Mere ideas found in a work cannot be protected by copyright and may be used freely. Accordingly, in order for copyright in a work to be infringed or violated, one has to copy the form in which the ideas are expressed. The mere use of the ideas found in a work does not represent a copyright violation.

For example, any person is entitled to write a book explaining to the general public how to use a recent version of a computer program. Such an idea cannot be appropriated by the person who first wrote the book. Hence the author could not prevent anyone from publishing a book on the same topic. But subsequent authors writing on the same topic should refrain from copying from books published or written before or by others.

The distinction between protected expressions and unprotected ideas has important practical consequences. It means that copyright does not preclude others from using *information* revealed in an author's work. For example, the author of a chess guide will be protected against the making and selling by others of copies of her book. This protection will not, however, prevent anyone from applying the instructions given therein when playing chess. Likewise, copyright does not protect the *underlying idea* after which certain works are created. The copyright in the famous Mickey Mouse concerns, for instance, only the specific features of that particular cartoon character, but does not give any exclusivity over the general idea to create artistic works about talking mice or other animals. The same holds finally true for an artist's characteristic *style or method*. Everyone may therefore make paintings in the cubist style developed by Picasso or in the dotty manner of French impressionists. And only if a concrete work of some of these

部作品的保护适用于思想的表达。作品中单纯的思想并不受版权的保护，可以自由使用。从而，一个人对思想的表现形式进行复制就构成侵犯和破坏版权。但仅仅对一部作品的思想加以利用不认为是侵犯版权。

例如，任何人都有权著书向大众解释如何使用最新版本的计算机程序。这一思想并不专属于第一位写书的人，所以作者不能禁止他人就同样的主题出版著作。但是，后来的作者在就同样主题写作时，对前人或者他人已发表或者写成的著作不得进行抄袭。

受保护的表达和不受保护的思想之间的区别具有很重要的实践影响。它意味着版权并不妨碍他人利用作者作品里揭示的信息。例如，一本受版权保护的国际象棋指南的作者可以制止他人制作或者销售她著作的复制品。但是，这种保护并不能阻止别人在下国际象棋时使用这些书中的教导。同样的，版权对创造作品所依据的思想也不予保护。例如，著名的米老鼠的版权只涉及这一特定的卡通角色的特征，对于谈论老鼠或其他别的动物而创作的艺术作品的一般想法并不具有专有权。对于艺术家独特的风格和方法最终也按同样的原则处理。任何人都可以沿用毕加索所创立的立体派风格或法国印象派的涂鸦方式来绘画。但是只有当这

painters is reproduced will copyright be infringed. Other examples of ideas that are not eligible for copyright protection include scientific theories, marketing concepts and algorithms.

In order to illustrate what kind of works may be protected, most copyright laws contain an elaborate, but usually not exhaustive, list of examples. The enumerated categories comprise typically works of language (such as writings and speeches); musical works (with or without text, such as songs, sonatas, music score made for films); dramatic works (such as plays, including pantomimes and choreographies); works of fine art (such as paintings, drawings, sculptures, including works of architecture and of applied art); photographic works and works of cinematography; illustrations of a scientific or technical nature (such as plans, maps and sketches). It is important to note that such lists are given by way of example only, and that other sorts of creations not specifically mentioned in the list may be protected provided they qualify for copyright, i. e. are original. The question then arises of when a work does qualify for protection. In other terms what is originality?

The Idea-Expression Dichotomy
• Copyright requires an expression in a particular form
• No protection of underlying ideas, mere information or style
• Usually non-exhaustive list of examples

When does a work qualify for copyright protection? The condition of originality

The central requirement for a work to qualify for copyright protection

些画家的具体作品被复制时，才对版权构成侵犯。另外一些不适用版权保护的思想包括科学理论、营销理念和算法。

为了说明何种作品应受版权保护，大多数版权法通常都列出了范例清单，但清单并不是包揽无遗的。通常列举出的范畴包括典型的语言类作品（如书面作品和演说）、音乐作品（例如附加或者不附加歌词的歌曲、奏鸣曲、为电影制作的配乐）、戏剧作品（例如戏剧，包括哑剧和舞蹈）、美术作品（例如绘画、素描、雕塑，包括建筑艺术作品和实用艺术作品）、摄影作品和电影作品、自然科学技术类的插图（例如平面图、地图和略图）。这类清单只能用例举的方式，清单中未例举的其他创作，只要符合版权的独创性要求，就可以得到保护。随之而来的问题是，什么时候一部作品才具备保护条件呢？换言之，什么是原创性？

思想表达的两分法
• 版权要求具有特定形式的表达
• 对所依据的思想、单纯的信息或风格不予以保护
• 通常是非穷尽的列举清单

作品什么时候才符合版权保护的要求？原创性的条件

一部作品享有版权保护的核心条件是其原创性。但原创性的

is that it must be original. There is no unanimity with regard to what originality means, nor universally agreed upon standards. Broadly speaking countries divide into two general categories. In common law countries courts require from the author that she displays some degree of skill, labour, and judgment, for her work to qualify as original (this is called the "sweat of the brow theory"). In civil law countries courts require more: in order to be original, a work must reflect the individual personality of its creator. Mere display of skill, labour and judgment is not enough: the author must also show creativity. This difference of appreciation may lead to different results, as common law courts may be less severe in their assessment of originality. Hence it may happen that some works which would not qualify as original in civil law countries because of the lack of element of creativity may nevertheless be considered original in common law countries if the author has shown a sufficient degree of skill, labour and judgment.

Despite the differences that characterise the concept of originality, one has to acknowledge that a far greater unanimity prevails concerning the issue of what is *not* required for copyright protection: that is to say that quality, novelty, artistic merit or value are no relevant criteria for judging whether a work is original or not. A work may be strongly criticised for its contents and condemned for its style by specialists and the general public, it will however not lose copyright protection. Finally, it does not matter what purpose a work has been created for, be it utilitarian or purely cultural: a piece of music made for the purpose of advertisement would qualify for protection in the same manner as a sonata or symphony.

Finally, one should note that a work might be protected as original even though it is based on a pre-existing work. Copyright also

含义是什么却没有一致的看法，也没有一致的标准。通常所有的国家都可以被划入两大法系。在普通法国家，法院需要作者在某种程度上显示出技巧、劳动和判断，以表明其作品是具有原创性（这也被称为“额头出汗理论”）。在大陆法系国家，法院对原创性有更高的要求：为了具有原创性，一部作品必须反映其创作人的个性。仅仅展示技巧、劳动和判断是不够的：作者还必须展示出其创造性。不同的评价可能带来不同的结果，普通法法院在对原创性的评估上可能稍微宽松些。所以，一些作品尽管在普通法系国家由于作者充分展示其技巧、劳动和判断而被认为具有独创性，但也可能因为缺少创造性因素而在大陆法系国家被认为不符合原创性的标准。

尽管原创性概念特点有所不同，但是不得不承认，质量、新颖性、艺术才华或价值并不是判断作品是否具有原创性的标准。一部作品有可能因为其内容和风格而受到专家和社会大众的批评和谴责，但却不会因此而丧失版权保护。最后，无论一部作品的创作目的是什么，无论是出于功利目的，还是纯粹文化意义上的目的，都与版权保护无关：为广告而作的音乐与奏鸣曲或交响乐同样受到保护。

最后，人们应注意到在已有作品的基础之上进行创作的作品仍然作为具有原创性的作品而受到保护。版权对“派生作品”也

protects "derivative works": translations, adaptations, arrangements of music and other alterations of a literary or artistic work receive the same protection as original works. So do collections of literary and artistic works, such as encyclopaedias and anthologies provided they are original by reason of the selection or arrangements of their contents.

For both derivative works and collections, the protection is granted "without prejudice to the copyright" in the pre-existing work or in the work forming part of the collection. This means that an author of a translation should obtain authorization to translate the work from the author of the work to be translated. Likewise an author of an anthology of poems should obtain authorization to publish the selected poems from their respective authors.

The Originality Criteria in Copyright Law
• Central requirement of originality to be interpreted by courts
• Form, purpose, quality, novelty, artistic merit or commercial value not relevant
• Derivative works protected as original works

Does copyright require any formalities?

Nowadays, it is an almost universally accepted principle that the protection of author's rights flows automatically from the act of creation and does not depend on any formalities, such as registration or deposit of the work. In that respect, copyright differs considerably from most forms of industrial property protection, such as patents or trademarks which generally require an act of registration.

The absence of any formalities is enshrined in several international conventions. Today, only a small number of countries

给予保护：翻译作品、改编作品、音乐的整理和文学艺术作品的变更都作为原创性作品受到同样保护。所以对文学艺术作品进行汇编，例如百科全书和选集，只要是对其内容进行的节选和编排具有独创性，都同样受到版权保护。

对派生作品和汇编作品而言，其版权保护的授予不得有损于原始作品或者构成汇编部分的作品的版权。这意味着翻译作品的作者应该获得被翻译作品的作者的授权才能翻译。同样，诗歌选集的作者也要获得被选中诗歌的作者分别的授权才能出版。

版权法上原创性的标准
• 原创性的核心要求由法院来解释
• 与形式、目的、质量、新颖性、艺术才华或者商业价值无关
• 派生作品也作为具有原创性的作品受到保护

版权的获得需要任何手续吗？

现在，几乎普遍都采取因创作行为而对作者权利自动保护的原则，不需要任何手续如登记或者缴存样本。在这一方面，版权和工业产权的大部分保护形式有显著区别，例如专利或者商标通常是需要经过登记手续的。

无需办理任何手续的原则已经在好几个国际公约中得以确认。今天，连一个前述国际公约都未签署的国家为数很少。众所

are not signatories to at least one of these. The widely known (c) symbol, was introduced by the UNESCO-administered 1952 Universal Copyright Convention (UCC) in order to provide a simple prescribed form of copyright notice: this symbol, accompanied by the name of the copyright owner and the year of first publication, appearing on all copies of a copyrighted work, guarantees its protection in all UCC member countries, including those requiring compliance with formalities as a condition of protection.

Although mandatory registration has meanwhile been abolished almost everywhere, many national laws allow for a voluntary registration of works by the national copyright administration or similar body. Such registration can serve as valuable *prima facie* evidence in legal disputes.

Absence of Formalities in Copyright Law
• Absence of formalities enshrined in international conventions
• (c) sign introduced by Universal Copyright Convention (1952)
• Voluntary registration may serve as *prima facie* evidence

Must works be fixed in a tangible form to be protected?

The issue of whether a work requires to be fixed in a tangible form in order to be protected is not dealt with in a uniform way. Usually common law countries require that, in order to enjoy protection, the work must be fixed by any tangible, material means (for example it could be written on a piece of paper, or recorded on a cassette, a CD, a DVD, or stored on a floppy disk or on the computer hard disk), whereas countries with a civil law tradition do not have such a

周知，“（c）”这个符号，是联合国教科文组织管理下的 1952 年《世界版权公约》（UCC）所引入的，目的是提供一个简单的版权通告形式：这个符号，连同版权所有人的姓名、第一次出版的年代一道出现在版权作品的每一件复制品上，就保证作品在 UCC 所有成员国中受到保护，包括在那些要求履行某些手续作为获得保护条件的国家。

尽管强制登记现在几乎已为各国所废止，但是许多国内法还是允许到国家版权管理部门或者类似单位进行自愿登记。这种登记在出现法律纠纷时可作为有价值的初步证据。

版权法不需要手续
• 无需登记已经为国际公约所确认
• 1952 年《世界版权公约》引入“（c）”符号
• 自愿的登记可以作为初步证据

受保护的作品必须要固定于某种载体上吗？

一件作品是否必须固定于某种载体才予以保护的问题目前还没有统一的解决方法。一般来说，普通法系国家要求作品固定于某种物质载体上才予以保护（例如，作品可以写在纸上，或者录在磁带、CD、DVD 或者存储在软盘或计算机硬盘上），而具有大陆法传统的国家则没有这种要求。国际法对两种方式都认可。

requirement. International law allows for both ways.

Whether a work needs to be fixed in order to benefit from protection has important practical consequences, especially with regard to works of improvisation such as music, speeches or choreographies. If fixation is required, those works would not be protected until they are either recorded or transcribed. By contrast, in a country without fixation requirement, copyright protection takes effect from the very moment in which the work is created, i. e. when the improvised music or dance is performed or the speech is held.

Fixation Requirement in Copyright
• Fixation ≠ registration; necessity depends on national legislation
• Concerns ephemeral works (e. g. music, speeches, choreographies)
• Decisive for the moment from which on protection takes place

Are computer programs protected?

Conforming to recent amendments in international law, most countries nowadays recognise computer programs as eligible subject matter for protection under copyright. Computer programs are usually protected regardless of the language in which they are written, be it source code or object code. The term generally refers to a series of instructions used directly or indirectly in an information processing system and may include both application programs and operating systems. To be protected, it is irrelevant in what form the program is embodied; it may be written on paper or stored on a CD or in a computer memory.

为了从保护中受益，作品是否需要固定在载体上具有重要的实际意义，特别是对即席而作的作品如音乐、演讲或者舞蹈。如果需要固定，则作品在被录制或者录写之前得不到保护。与此相反，在一个不需要固定的国家，自作品创作完成之时，也就是当即席创作的音乐或舞蹈被表演或者演讲被演说之时起，版权保护即开始生效。

版权对固定于载体的要求
• 固定≠登记；必需依国内立法规定
• 短暂存在的作品（例如音乐、演讲、舞蹈）
• 决定保护生效的时刻

计算机程序受保护吗?

适应最近国际法上的修订，大部分国家现如今都承认计算机程序是版权保护的合格客体。通常计算机程序的保护与它是用哪种语言写成的无关，无论是用源代码，还是目标代码。计算机程序通常指在信息处理系统中直接或间接使用的一系列指令，包括应用程序和操作系统。保护与程序具体存储形式无关，它可以是写在纸上或存储在 CD 或计算机内存里。

The Protection of Computer Programs
• Includes applications and operating systems alike
• Applies to both source code and object code
• Form of embodiment (stored/written) irrelevant

How are databases protected?

The term "database" refers to an aggregate of information data, selected in accordance with certain constant principles, systematically arranged and stored in the memory of a computer system to which a number of users have access. Databases may be generally protected in two ways:

First of all, a database may be eligible for protection as an original intellectual creation by reason of the *selection or arrangement* of the information it contains. If such selection is original, protection follows. In that case we speak of original databases, which are essentially subject to the general copyright rules. The object of protection here is the distinctive *structure* of the database, i. e. the "architecture" given to it by the author, and not the *data or material* itself. Third parties may therefore use the same or similar data; yet they must not adopt the way in which the original database arranges them, nor the same selection.

Additionally, a number of countries have introduced a separate "*sui generis*" right (i. e. an independent right that protects databases outside the scope of copyright) for manufacturers of databases against extraction or re-utilisation of the *contents* themselves. As opposed to original databases, this form of protection may be obtained regardless

对计算机程序的保护
• 包括应用和操作系统
• 适用于源代码和目标代码
• 与具体形式（存储/写作）无关

数据库如何保护?

“数据库”这个术语指信息数据的集合，它是按照某些固定的原则选择出来，系统化排列和存储在计算机程序的内存里，使许多用户得以使用。数据库通常可以依两种方式保护：

首先，数据库可以因对其包含的信息进行选择和排列而作为原始智力创作从而得到保护。如果这种选择是原创性的，即得到保护。在这种情况下，我们称之为原始数据库，主要适用版权一般规则。此处保护的客体是数据库独特的结构，即作者赋予数据库的特殊结构，而不是数据和材料本身。第三人可以使用同样或者类似的数据，但是对这些数据的使用不能采取原始数据库的编排方式或同样的选择方式。

另外，许多国家引入了单独的“自成一类的”（sui generis）权利（在版权范围之外对数据库进行保护的独立权利），以保护数据库的制造者制止对其数据库内容的摘录或再次使用。与原创性数据库的要求相反，这种保护形式的获得不以数据库的结构或选择必须具有原创性为条件。此种保护方法的决定性因素是对搜

of whether the structure or selection is in itself original or not. The decisive element here is rather the investment of time, money and effort to collect the data or other materials.

Protection of Databases
• "Original" databases: protected as compilation by reason of structure
• *Sui generis* protection of contents of non-original databases

Can copyright protect traditional cultural expressions ("folklore")?

Traditional cultural expressions (sometimes also referred to as "folklore") such as the traditional music, stories and artistic designs of local communities, have been developed under vernacular laws and customs for generations. They often constitute an important part of the culture from which they originate and are at the same time linked to the promotion of cultural diversity and human creativity. Today, many local and indigenous communities are concerned with the increasing commercial exploitation of their heritage without due respect to their own cultural and economic interests.

The collective and anonymous nature of those expressions poses particular problems to the application of existing intellectual property rights, including copyright law. Though certain contemporary expressions may indeed meet the originality criteria, copyright as a genuinely individual right, rewarding personal creativity with a monopoly limited in time, may not in all cases prove to be the suitable framework for protection.

UNESCO, as well as a number of other international bodies, has

集数据或其他材料所投入的时间、资金和努力。

数据库的保护
• “原创性”数据库：因编辑其结构而获得保护
• 对于非原创性数据库内容的自成一类的保护

版权能保护传统文化表达（“民间文学艺术”）吗？

传统文化表达（有时也称为“民间文学艺术”），诸如地方社会的传统音乐、故事和艺术设计，在其本国法律和风俗下世代传承发展。它们往往构成母体文化的重要组成部分，并且同时与促进文化多样性和人类创造性相关联。今天，许多地区和土著群体对日益增长的对其传统遗产的商业利用而无视其文化和经济利益之状况深感忧虑。

这些表达的集体创作性和匿名性对于适用现存的知识产权包括版权带来了特殊问题。尽管某些当代的表达符合原创性标准，但是版权作为纯粹的个人权利，授予个人创造以一定时限的独占权，却无法证明在所有情况中都是一种适当的保护框架。

联合国教科文组织，与众多其他国际组织一道，在探索新的

been striving for more than two decades to explore possibilities of new forms of protection that are more specific, more operational and more practicable, and that will ultimately achieve a broad international consensus. Among UNESCO's activities is for instance the elaboration of the Model Provisions for National Laws on the Protection of Expressions of Folklore against Illicit Exploitation and other Prejudicial Actions in 1982 (together with WIPO), as well as the adoption of the Convention for the Safeguarding of the Intangible Cultural Heritage in 2003.

Traditional cultural expressions and Folklore
• Forming part of the culture from which they originate
• Impersonal/collective nature at odds with individual property right
• New forms of protection explored by UNESCO and others

保护形式方面已有 20 多年。新的保护形式要更独特、更具操作性和更具实践意义，并且最后还要达成广泛的国际共识。教科文组织开展了众多活动，例如 1982 年制定的《关于保护民间文学艺术表达反对非法利用和其他损害行为的示范法》（与 WIPO 一道），以及 2003 年通过的《无形文化遗产保护公约》。

传统文化表达和民间文学艺术
• 构成其渊源文化的一部分
• 非个人性/集体性与个人财产权不同
• 联合国教科文组织和其他组织对新型保护方式的探索

Copyright Ownership

Introduction

Basically, there is not much discussion that copyright in a work will initially belong to the person who has created it, i. e. the author. However, there are exceptions to this rule, which are explained below.

One should also point out that ownership of copyright may be transferred, whether by way of inheritance after death or through contractual agreements.

Copyright Ownership
• Initial ownership generally vested in author
• Certain exceptions in particular cases
• Copyright transferable after death or by contracts

Who is the "author"?

In the simplest and most frequent case, the author is the natural person who has created the work. Approach in national copyright laws vary however, with regard to the definition of authorship in cases when third parties get involved.

Many laws, especially in common-law countries, apply rather

版权所有权

引言

一部作品的版权最初属于创作它的人即作者，这一点基本没什么争论。但是，这一规则有例外，下面将对其进行说明。

同时，也应该指出版权所有权是可以转移的，无论是通过死后遗产继承还是通过契约达成协议。

版权所有权
• 作者通常被授予最初的所有权
• 在特定的情况中有一定的例外
• 版权可在死亡后或者通过契约转移

谁是“作者”？

在最简单和最常见的情况下，作者就是创作作品的自然人。但是当第三方介入时，对作者身份的定义在各国版权法上则有不同的规定。

许多法律，特别是普通法国家的法律，规定宽泛的标准允许

wide criteria which allow initial copyright ownership to be vested in persons other than the actual creator. For example, copyright may, since the first instance of the creation of the work, belong to a corporate body or legal entity, which are deemed to be the "author" by virtue of a legal fiction. This becomes especially important in the case of works made for hire (see next question).

By contrast, the European continental legal tradition, as a rule, attaches authorship inseparably to the person who has created the work. This means, at least when the principle is strictly followed, that only human beings or natural persons can be the initial owners of copyright in literary or artistic works. Unlike in common-law countries, legal entities cannot be indicated as authors since they do not have the capacity to create works. Therefore, legal entities will need to acquire rights in the work subsequently, by contract.

Who is the "Author"?
• Primarily the natural person who created the work
• Common law: third parties may be deemed authors
• Continental tradition: no author apart from the creator

Who owns the rights in a work made for hire?

According to the common law legal tradition, when an employee produces a work in the normal course of her employment, the employer is regarded as the initial owner of copyright in the work, and hence considered the author, unless there has been an express agreement to the contrary. The justification behind this lies in the fact that the employer is the one who makes the decisions and takes the

把最初的版权所有权授予其他人而不是实际的创作人。例如，作品首创之后，版权可以属于法人团体或法律实体，它们因法律拟制而成为作者。这一点在受雇佣而创作的作品的情况下尤其重要（参见下一个问题）。

与此相反，在欧洲大陆法律传统中，原则上作者身份与创作作品的人不可分离。这就意味着至少当严格遵守这一原则时，只有人类或者自然人能够成为文学艺术作品的最初版权拥有者。与普通法国家不同，法律实体因不具有创作作品的能力而不被认为是作者。因此，法律实体只能在以后通过契约来获得作者的权利。

谁是“作者”？
● 首先是创作作品的自然人
● 普通法：第三方可以被视为作者
● 大陆法传统：作者不能与创作人分离

谁拥有雇佣作品的权利？

按照普通法法律传统，当一位受雇佣者在其正常受雇过程中创造出作品时，其雇主被视为作品最初版权的拥有者，也即被认为是作者，除非有相反的特别协议。其背后的理由在于雇主是作

initiatives, who pays for the work and for its production. Therefore she should reap all the economic benefits that are derived from it.

In countries where copyright laws attach authorship solely to natural persons, the approach is different: rights are vested initially in the employee and the employer (whether a natural person or a legal entity, such as a company) who hired the employee may subsequently acquire rights in a work by virtue of a contract.

Works made for hire
• Typical for common-law tradition
• Applies to works produced in the course of employment
• Copyright initially vested in employer instead of employee

Who owns copyright in anonymous or pseudonymous works?

Copyright laws generally acknowledge that there are cases where a person may wish to publish a work without revealing her name (anonymously) or under a borrowed or pen-name (pseudonymous). In most countries, it is the publisher who exercises copyright in such works on behalf of the author, except in the case of "*transparent pseudonyms*" which leave no doubt as to the identity of the authors and are therefore equivalent to the latter's real names (e.g. Georges Sand, Molière).

Yet, it should be clearly understood that in these cases, the publisher is not the real owner of copyright but is only entitled to protect and enforce the author's rights by virtue of a legal fiction following which the publisher is presumed to represent the author. Once the real author reveals his or her true identity, this presumption

出决定和提出倡议的人，她为作品及其创作支付了报酬。因此她有权利获得所有的源于作品的经济利益。

在版权法只把自然人视为作者的国家里，又有不同的规定：权利最初被授予受雇佣者，雇主（无论是自然人还是法律实体，例如公司）即雇佣受雇人的人可以在以后通过契约获得作品的权利。

受雇佣创造的作品
• 典型的普通法传统
• 适用于雇佣过程中创作的作品
• 版权最初授予雇主而非受雇佣者

谁拥有匿名或者笔名作品的版权?

版权法通常都承认人们可以不披露本人姓名（匿名作品）或者使用借用名或笔名（笔名作品）来发表作品。在大多数国家，都是由出版商代表作者行使这些作品的版权，除非是在“透明笔名”的情况下，也即对作者的身份认定毫无疑义并且笔名即等同于作者真名（例如乔治桑、莫里哀）。

然而，人们要明确认识到在匿名或笔名发表作品的情况下，出版商并非版权的真实所有人，而只是基于法律拟制的被推定代表作者而有权保护和行使作者权利。一旦真正的作者披露了他或她的真实身份，则这种推定就不再具有效力。此后，出版商即从游戏中出局，权利的行使仅由作者本人来进行，除非他或她将权

will no longer be valid. From that moment on, the publisher steps out of the game and the rights are exercised solely by the author, unless transferred by him or her to a third party.

Copyright in Anonymous and Pseudonymous Works
• Legal presumption in favour of publishers
• Valid until the author reveals his or her identity

Who owns the rights in works created by several persons?

Two or more persons can collaborate to the creation of a work in different ways. Copyright ownership in such works follows different rules according to the degree in which the individual contributions can be distinguished within the final result.

When the contributions are done with the intention to be merged into an inseparable or interdependent unit we speak of "joint works" (or "works of collaboration"). Such is the case, for example, when two authors join their efforts to write a book together. However, if the book is written by one author and another one contributes a specific chapter and is given credit for this chapter, then this would not be a joint work because the contributions are not inseparable or interdependent.

In the cases of joint works, the contributors are considered as co-authors who jointly own the rights in their creation. As joint owners they must generally exercise their rights together. Basically, co-authors may not unreasonably refuse to give their consent for the exploitation of the work. Unless otherwise contractually stipulated,

利转让给第三方。

匿名和笔名作品的版权
●法律推定由出版商行使版权
●在作者披露其身份前一直有效

数人创作的作品版权由谁拥有?

二人或多人可合作以不同方式创作作品。此类作品的版权所有要依照不同规则，按照在最后结果中个人贡献程度来确定。

当作品出于合成一个不可分割或相互依存的单元的意图而完成时，我们称之为“合著”（或合作作品）。例如两位作者共同撰写一本书。但是，如果书由一位作者所写，另一位作者对特定章节作出贡献并因这一章节受到赞许时，就不是合著作品了，因为各自的贡献不再是密不可分或相互依存的。

在合著作品中作出贡献的人被认为是共同作者，对他们的创作共同享有权利。作为共同的所有人，他们必须共同行使他们的权利。基本上，共同作者都不会不合理地拒绝同意对其作品进行使用。除另有规定外，应当等额分配收益。

profits are distributed in equal parts.

Joint works are to be distinguished from "composite works". The latter term is used if two or more pre-existing works are linked to a new creation without losing their individual character. For example, when music is written on pre-existing lyrics, and thus a song is created, both the music and the lyrics may be used separately from the song, without affecting the rights in the new "composite" work. In that case, while the rights in this new work (the song) are held jointly, copyright in the individual contributions (the music and the lyrics) continues as a rule to belong to the respective creators, subject to specific contractual arrangements which may have been made.

Finally, a "collective work" merely assembles several contributions without amounting to a joint work. Among the examples of collectives works are periodicals, anthologies and encyclopaedias as well as, to a certain extent, databases. Though the contributions in this case are separate and discernible, they are often undertaken at the initiative of someone who plans, arranges, coordinates, prepares and publishes the collection (often called the "editor"). It is therefore generally recognized that, without prejudice to the copyright in the individual works, there is a separate copyright in the whole, which is usually vested in this person or legal entity.

合著作品与“合成作品”是有区别的。后者是将事先存在的两部或多部作品在不丧失其个性特征的前提下连接成为一项新作品。例如，为已存在的歌词谱上乐曲而创作出一首歌曲，但乐曲和歌词都可以从歌曲中分离出来使用，而对新的“合成作品”的权利不产生影响。在此种情况下，新作品（歌曲）的权利是共同享有的，而单独的组成部分（音乐和抒情诗）的版权依照规定仍属于其分别的创造者，除非合同中另有规定。

最后，“集合作品”仅仅是集合了几个单独部分，并不构成共同作品。集合作品的例子，诸如期刊、选集和百科全书，在某种程度上包括数据库。尽管在此种情况下各组成部分是可分离的和可辨别的，但是作品的完成是由于那些计划、安排、协调、准备和出版集合作品的人（通常称为“主编”）的倡导。通常认为整体作品的版权属于主编人或法律实体，而不损害单独作品的版权。

Works Created by Several Persons		
Joint works	Composite works	Collective Works
Contributions merged into an inseparable or interdependent unit ↓ —Joint copyright in new work for all contributors	Pre-existing works linked to a new creation ↓ —Copyrights in pre-existing works remain separate —Joint copyright in new work for all contributors	Merely assemble several contributions ↓ —Copyrights in contributions remain separate Copyright in collection for the editor

Who owns the rights in cinematographic works?

The vast number of contributors to a film production poses particular challenges for copyright laws. Depending on which legal tradition a country follows, two basic solutions to the question of copyright ownership of cinematographic works may be found in domestic laws.

In countries adhering to the civil law legal tradition, the copyright in a film belongs generally to several physical persons, who have contributed to the creation of the work. The models, however, may vary considerably from one country to another. In some cases, films are considered as joint works of a number of co-authors (such as the director, the script writer, the cameraman and the music composer) who jointly own the copyright in the overall work. Other countries only consider the director as the author of the film and grant, according to the rules for composite works, a separate copyright for each of the other creative contributions. In either case, the producer must enter into contractual arrangements with every right-owner before the commercial exploitation of the film may take place.

数人创作的作品		
合作作品	合成作品	集合作品
各部分融合成一个密不可分或相互依存的单一体 ↓ ——合作作品的版权归所有撰稿人	事先存在的作品联合成新作 ↓ ——事先存在的作品版权仍单独保留 ——新作品的共同版权归全体	仅仅将数个部分汇总而成新作品 ↓ ——各部分版权仍分别保有集合作品版权归主编

电影作品的版权归谁?

一部电影作品有为数众多的创作者，这给版权法提出了特殊的挑战。依照一个国家遵循的法律传统，在各国国内法中可以找到电影作品版权归属问题的两个基本解决方案。

在继承大陆法传统的国家里，电影版权通常归属于对创作电影作出贡献的那些自然人。但是这一模式在国与国之间也有很大的区别。有些情况下，电影被认为是许多共同作者（诸如导演、编剧、摄影师和作曲者）的合作作品，他们就整体作品共同拥有版权。另外一些国家则只承认导演是电影的作者，然后按照合成作品的规定授予其他创作部分以单独的版权。无论何种情况，在对电影进行商业利用之前，制片人必须和每位版权所有人达成协议安排。

By contrast, copyright laws following the common law tradition usually consider the producer of a film as the sole copyright owner. The same goes as far as works made for hire are concerned, the individual contributors are basically not granted any rights. Even where some rights are conferred to the principal collaborators (such as the rights that the UK copyright legislation grants to the film director), they are usually quite limited in scope and their application is subject to a number of conditions. The rationale behind this approach is to facilitate the film's entry into the market by avoiding cumbersome negotiations with numerous right owners.

Rights Ownership in Cinematographic Works
• Continental laws: films as joint or composite works, several right owners
• Common law: approach: producer typically sole copyright owner

相反，遵循普通法传统的国家里，其版权法通常将电影的制片人作为惟一的版权所有人。正如同雇佣作品的情况一样，每个对作品作出贡献的人基本不享有任何权利。即使某些权利被授予主要的合作者（例如英国版权法授权给电影导演），他们通常在范围上要受到相当限制并且行使时要满足一系列条件。这种方式背后的理由是为了避免与众多权利所有者进行繁重的谈判从而便利电影进入市场。

电影作品的权利归属
• 大陆法：电影作为合作作品或合成作品有数个权利人
• 普通法：方式：制片人是典型的惟一版权所有人

The Moral Rights of Authors

Introduction

As a creation of the mind, the work reflects the author's personality. Therefore, apart from economic considerations, the author may also have interests in her work which are not strictly financial or pecuniary, such as the right to claim authorship and to object to derogatory uses. Prerogatives like these are referred to as the author's *moral rights*, as opposed to his or her economic rights.

Partially by virtue of international treaties, most copyright laws in the world have today embraced the notion of moral rights, though scope and implementation of these rights still vary considerably from one country to another. International law requires recognition of two kinds of moral rights: the right of attribution (or the right to claim authorship) and the right of integrity. But many national legislations grant the author other moral rights as well, such as the right to choose whether the work should be published or not, usually referred to as the right of disclosure, and the right of withdrawal.

The Moral Rights of Authors
• Concerns the author's non-pecuniary interests
• Recognized in most countries with different modalities
• Recognition required by international law

作者的精神权利

引言

作为思维的创造，作品反映作者的人格。所以，诸如作者身份权和反对损毁使用作品权等权利都不是严格意义上的财务金钱性质的权利。作者除经济上的考虑外，对其作品还享有一些像上面所谈到的非经济性的利益。此类特权被称做作者的精神权利，与作者的经济权利不同。

当今世界大多数版权法都部分地依据国际条约接受精神权利的概念，尽管国与国之间规定的权利范围和实施状况有很大的差别。国际法要求承认两种精神权利：作品归属权（或者表明作者身份权）和维护作品完整权。但许多国内立法还同时授予作者以其他精神权利，诸如决定作品是否出版权，这通常指发表作品权和撤销权。

作者的精神权利
• 涉及作者的非金钱利益
• 多数国家承认不同的模式
• 国际法要求承认精神权利

The Most Important Moral Rights
• Right of attribution (authorship)
• Right of integrity
• Right of disclosure
• Right of withdrawal

How has recognition of moral rights evolved internationally?

Originally moral rights are to be linked to the theories that base copyright on natural law and personal rights. It is hence no surprise that these rights are more specifically highlighted in countries where civil law traditions prevail. From this perspective it is worth noting that moral rights were first recognized in France, during the first half of the 19th century, under the expression "*droit moral*". That explains the origin of the expression "moral rights". By contrast, moral rights are viewed with less favour in common law countries, where emphasis has traditionally been put on the investment embodied in the work.

The 1928 revision of the Berne Convention (the "Rome Act") was a decisive step towards the international recognition of moral rights, as it introduced an obligation for the contracting states to provide protection for the rights of attribution and integrity. Today, these rights are enshrined in the famous Article 6*bis* of the Berne Convention. Subsequent international instruments, such as the WIPO Treaties of 1996, have also made room for moral rights.

In practical terms this Berne Convention requirement means that, at the moment of its accession to Convention, every country, including

最重要的精神权利
• 归属权（作者身份权）
• 保护作品完整权
• 发表权
• 撤销权

精神权利的承认在国际范围内是如何发展的？

最初的精神权利是与自然法版权理论与个人权利理论相联系的。所以，这些权利在大陆法传统的国家里得到特别的重视也就不奇怪了。值得注意的是，这些精神权利是首先在法国得到认可的，在19世纪上半叶，法国出现了"精神权利"（droit moral）的表述。这就是"精神权利"这一表述的起源。与此相反，在普通法国家里，精神权利受到的关注要小得多。在那里，传统上更强调的是对作品的投资。

1928年对《伯尔尼公约》的修订（罗马文本）朝着在国际上承认精神权利方面迈出了决定性的一步。它规定了各缔约国在归属权和作品完整权的保护方面的义务。今天，这些权利规定在《伯尔尼公约》著名的第6条之二中。随后的国际文件，例如1996年世界知识产权组织的两个条约也对精神权利作出规定。

就实践而言，《伯尔尼公约》的这项要求意味着在加入公约时，所有缔约国，包括属于普通法系的国家，都应在其国内法中

those belonging to the common law family, should have expressly introduced protection of moral rights in its domestic law. Yet, since the Convention leaves it to contracting states to determine the way in which they will give effect to their international obligations, some legislations have considered it sufficient to afford protection of these rights mainly on a basis, different from copyright law, for instance under tort and contract law.

Development of International Recognition
• Originally characteristic of civil law systems
• Art. 6*bis* Berne Convention / 1996 WIPO Treaties
• Implementation outside copyright possible

What are the basic features of moral rights?

Moral rights are by their very nature, connected to the person of the author, they are not property rights. This explains why, contrary to economic rights, they are not assignable. An author cannot transfer her moral right to someone else, whereas she would be allowed to sell her economic rights. Some countries however, especially those adhering to the common law system, allow the waiver (or renunciation) of moral rights under certain conditions.

The close link that exists between moral rights and the author also explains the provision of the Berne Convention to the effect that moral rights exist independently of economic rights. This means that moral rights remain with the author who will be entitled to exercise them even though she has transferred her economic rights to someone else. For example, an author may have transferred to a publisher her right to

明确规定对精神权利的保护。然而由于公约授权各缔约国决定它们承担国际义务的方式，因而一些国家的立法认为通过与版权法不同的法律，例如侵权法与合同法，就可以对这些权利提供足够的保护。

国际承认的发展
• 最初属于大陆法系的特征
• 《伯尔尼公约》第 6 条之二/1996 年世界知识产权组织的两个条约
• 在版权之外可能实施的保护

什么是精神权利的基本特点？

精神权利依其本身特性与作者个人相联系，它们不是财产权。这就可以解释为什么它与经济权利不同，精神权利是不可转让的。一位作者不能把她的精神权利转让给其他人，但是她可以卖掉她的经济权利。然而，某些国家，特别在一些普通法系国家，允许在一定条件下放弃（或抛弃）精神权利。

这种精神权利和作者之间的紧密联系也可以解释《伯尔尼公约》的下述规定，即精神权利独立于经济权利而存在。这就意味着作者即使转让了她的经济权利但仍然可以保有行使精神权利。例如，一位作者可以把她的小说的复制权和发行权转让给出版商，但是，这无关于她所继续拥有的精神权利。她仍然可以在小

reproduce and distribute her novel. Yet, that has no bearing on the destiny of moral rights which continue to belong to her. She may hence claim authorship in the novel and the publisher may not remove her name, as the author of the work, or substitute it with another one.

For how long should moral rights be protected? This issue has traditionally given rise to controversy. While common law countries, as a rule, tend to provide that moral rights will not be protected after the author's death, the civil law tradition generally regards moral rights as perpetual: in this case the rights in question may be exercised posthumously by the author's heirs or, as provided under some national laws, by certain public or private bodies for the benefit of a country's cultural heritage. The Berne Convention contains a compromise that the rights granted under its Article 6*bis* should last for *at least* as long as the author's economic rights. Today, many Member States have adopted this model and grant the same term of protection for both moral and economic rights. Under international standards, the term of protection for economic rights is 50 years after the death of the author but a few countries extend the term of protection to 70 years *post mortem*.

Basic Features of Moral Rights
• Exist independently from economic rights
• Generally not assignable
• Duration at least as long as economic rights

What does the right of attribution stand for?

The right of attribution is one of the moral rights provided under Article 6*bis* of the Berne Convention. It is often referred to as the "paternity" right, which alludes to the spiritual kinship between the

说中宣布她的作者身份，并且出版商也不能删除她的名字或者用其他人的名字代替，因为她是作品的作者。

精神权利的保护期应该有多长呢？这个问题长久以来一再被争论。普通法国家通常倾向于作者死亡后就不保护精神权利，大陆法传统国家通常认为精神权利是永恒的：作者死亡后由其继承人行使精神权利或者如某些国家立法所规定，由某些公众团体或私人团体为了国家文化遗产的利益而行使作者的精神权利。《伯尔尼公约》第 6 条之二中对规定的精神权利作了折中的处理，其期限至少要和作者的经济权利保护期一样长。今天，许多成员国已经接受了这一模式，并对经济权利和精神权利给予同样的保护期限。按照国际标准，对经济权利的保护为作者终身及其死后 50 年，但是少数国家将保护期延长到作者去世后 70 年。

精神权利的基本特点
• 独立于经济权利而存在
• 通常不可转让
• 保护期至少等同于经济权利

归属权意味着什么？

归属权是《伯尔尼公约》的第 6 条之二赋予的一项精神权利。它经常被称为“家父”权，暗指在作者和作品之间的精神血缘关系，尽管这一术语今天似乎已经过时了。

work and its creator, though this terminology may today seem outdated.

The attribution right reserves for the author the decision of whether or not to associate her name with the work and of when the work will be published or otherwise made available to the public. It hence consists in the right to claim authorship, as well as to remain anonymous. Under the attribution right the author may also use a borrowed name (a pseudonym), like the author of "Alice's Adventures in Wonderland", who was born as Charles Lutwidge Dodgson, but is known to the world as Lewis Carroll. Alternatively, the author may decide to use an acronym (like the famous "AD" of the early 16th century German painter *Albrecht Dürer*) . Along with this prerogative goes the obligation of users to acknowledge the source and the name of the author, when they make quotations or otherwise refer to a work.

The right of the author to be recognized as such has to be distinguished from the right to object to any wrongful attribution of authorship, e. g. when the signature of a famous artist is imitated on a painting, which is not of her making. The possibility to defend one's name against usurpation by third parties does not, strictly speaking, fall within the category of authors' moral rights but rather forms a part of the general category of personality rights, to which every individual is entitled, regardless of whether she is an author or not.

The Right of Attribution
• Right to claim authorship in a work
• ≠ Right against wrongful attribution

Against what acts does the right of integrity protect?

The right of integrity allows the author to prevent any distortion,

归属权为作者保留了是否在其作品上署名以及何时出版或以其他方式向公众提供其作品的权利。它还包括明确作者身份的权利，当然也可以匿名。在归属权下作者可以使用借用名（笔名），如《爱丽斯仙境漫游记》的作者本来的姓名是 Charles Lutwidge Dodgson，但在全世界都以 Lewis Carroll 而闻名。另外，作者也可以决定使用缩略字（像著名的 16 世纪的“AD”，即德国画家 Albrecht Durer）。除上述情况外，使用者在引用或参考作品时必须要表明作品的来源和作者的姓名。

此类作者权与反对错误署名的权利是有区别的，后者例如在其创作的绘画上模仿一位著名艺术家的签名。保护一个人的名字防止被第三方冒用，从严格意义上说并非属于作者精神权利的范畴，而是人身权利的一部分。任何人都有这种权利，不论其是否是作者。

归属权
• 在作品中表明作者身份
• ≠反对错误署名权

保护作品完整权反对何种行为?

作品完整权允许作者制止任何歪曲、篡改或毁损作品从而损

mutilation or derogatory action in relation to the work that would be prejudicial to her honour or reputation. This prerogative reflects the fact that the author's personality is intimately reflected in the work. It is therefore also often called the "right to respect".

The integrity right grants protection against unauthorized modifications (a publisher may not, for instance, strike out chapters from a narrative), as well as against use of the work in a demeaning context (an example would be the publication of a piece of lyrics in a pornographic magazine). With the advance of digital technology, authors face new types of threats to their works' integrity as it becomes easier and easier to shred a work into its components at will.

Yet, not every deviation from the author's original design must be necessarily held to constitute an infringement of the integrity right. The problem becomes especially delicate in the case of adaptations. For example, when a novel is turned into a movie, the new medium or form of expression may make certain changes inevitable. Article 6*bis* of the Berne Convention is rather elastic in this regard as it would allow some changes or modifications to be brought to a work but only to the extent that they are not prejudicial to the author's honour or reputation. Many national legislations have therefore made the integrity right subject to a balance of the legitimate interests of all parties concerned.

The Right of Integrity
• Right to prevent derogatory use of the work
• Takes into account both content and context
• Exercise often subject to balance of interest

害作者名誉或荣誉的行为，这种权利反映出一个事实，即作者的人格深刻地反映在其作品中，所以也被称为“受尊重权”。

保护作品完整权可以制止未经授权的修改（例如一位出版商不能从一篇故事中删除几章）以及制止在贬低的意义上使用作品（例如将抒情诗歌印制在色情杂志上）。伴随着数字技术的进步，作者们面临着对其作品完整性的新类型的威胁，因为作品越来越容易随意地分解为各个部分。

但是，并非每一个偏离作者最初设想的行为都构成对完整权的侵害。这一问题在改编的情况下尤为微妙。例如，当一部小说被改编为电影，新的媒体或表达形式可能造成一些不可避免的改变。《伯尔尼公约》第6条之二很有弹性，它允许对作品作一些改动或修正，但以不损害作者荣誉或名誉的程度为限。因而许多国内立法也规定完整权以平衡各相关方的合法利益。

完整权
• 制止贬低性使用作品的权利
• 考虑到内容和上下文关系
• 常用来平衡各方面利益

When does the right of disclosure apply?

Under the right of disclosure the author is entitled to decide whether her work is to be made available to the public for the first time, and if so, in what form and way and under what terms and conditions. This prerogative comprises the revelation of the work's content as well as the publication of a description. In certain countries, the right of disclosure may go as far as allowing an author to prevent her work from being divulged to the public if for personal reasons she is not satisfied with it, and this in spite of a contractual agreement that she may have entered into. For instance, in an early case at the end of the 19th century in France, the famous painter James McNeill Whistler was allowed not to deliver to the commissioner a portrait with which he was dissatisfied.

It is important to note that bringing the work to the attention of others does not, in itself, constitute disclosure. Disclosure rather requires a divulgation beyond the author's private circle of family and friends. For instance, the staging of a play at a private family gathering will not constitute disclosure, unlike the staging of the same play by the local theatre group, and this irrespective of the number of viewers.

The right of disclosure is not provided for in the Berne Convention and is recognized mainly in countries that belong to the civil law tradition.

The Right of Disclosure
• Relates to making the work publicly known
• Work may not be divulged despite contract
• Requires divulgation beyond the private circle

发表权何时行使?

依发表权，作者有权决定是否首次向公众提供其作品以及以何种形式、方式和条件提供其作品。这一权利包含披露作品的内容，以及将叙述的情节予以出版。在某些国家，发表权甚至允许作者因为对其作品感到不满意的个人原因而制止向公众发表其作品，即使作者已经签订了合同性的协议。例如：19 世纪末的法国有一个早期案例，著名画家 James McNeill Whistler 被允许不把他所不满意的画像提交给政府官员。

需要指出，使其作品引起他人注意，其本身并不构成发表。这一点是很重要的。发表需要在作者私人家庭和朋友圈子以外公布。例如，在私人家庭集会中的舞台剧不构成发表，这与在当地剧院里公演同样的戏剧是不一样的，并且与观众的数量多少无关。

发表权在《伯尔尼公约》中没有规定，主要为大陆法系国家所承认。

发表权
• 与使作品广为公众知晓有关
• 作品即便有契约也可以不发表
• 需要超出私人圈子范围以外发表

What is the right of withdrawal?

It may sometimes happen that, the author's thoughts or opinions on issues exposed in the work change and that the work no longer reflects her intellectual or artistic views. In case this occurs after the work has been lawfully brought to the public, the author cannot resort to the disclosure right to prevent it from being distributed. Yet, some copyright laws grant to the author the right to withdraw the work from the market.

Since the withdrawal affects the interests of those who have already acquired the right to use the work (for example the publisher of the work, who is entitled to make and distribute copies of the work), the right of withdrawal is normally subject to a range of conditions. Such conditions are designed to take into account the legitimate interests of the persons who have entered into contractual agreements with the author. Typically, they are entitled to indemnification for their resulting losses. Moreover, some laws provide that the original contractors will enjoy priority for the conclusion of a new contract, should the author decide to resume the exploitation of the work.

The Right to Withdraw
• The author may withdraw the work after change of ideas
• Subject to conditions to protect third parties

什么是撤销权?

有时会发生这样的事情，作者在作品中阐述问题的思想或观点改变了，并且作品也不再反映其思想或艺术观点。如果这种情况发生在作品已经合法地向公众披露之后，作者就不能诉诸发表权来阻止作品公之于众。但是，某些版权法却授予作者将作品从市场上撤回的权利。

因为撤销权影响那些已经获得作品使用权的人的利益（例如作品的出版商有权制作和发行作品的复制件），所以撤销权通常要符合一系列条件。这些条件要考虑到与作者订立契约性协议的人的合法利益。典型的条件是他们有权就所受损结果获偿。此外，某些法律还规定，若作者决定重新利用其作品，则最初的缔约者就新合同的缔结享有优先权。

撤销权
• 作者改变想法后可撤销作品
• 要符合保护第三方的条件

Economic Rights of Authors

Introduction

In contrast to moral rights, economic rights enable the author to earn a living from her creative work. In most cases, musicians, artists and other creators do not exercise their economic rights personally, but entrust professional partners such as book publishers or record producers to bring their works to the market.

Economic rights are generally exclusive rights. Practically speaking, this means two things. Firstly it is up to the right-owner to authorize the doing by others of an act which falls within the scope of her rights. Consequently, anyone who wishes to use a protected work in a way covered by the author's economic rights (for instance by publishing a novel, or recording a song), must seek the right owner's authorization to that effect. The latter can thus determine the conditions of the use, including the remuneration.

Secondly, the author also has the right not to grant permission to the would-be user (right of refusal). In this case should the user proceed with her activity (for example perform in public a play for which authorization has been refused), she may be sued for copyright violation.

It may be worth mentioning that economic rights are not always of an exclusive nature. In some instances national legislations as well as international treaties allow that uses be made of the work in some situations, without having to seek or obtain authorization from the

作者的经济权利

引言

与精神权利相反，经济权利使作者得以凭其创作作品谋生。大多数情况下，音乐家、艺术家和其他创作人并不亲自行使其经济权利，而是委托职业伙伴诸如书籍出版商或录音制作人将其作品投放市场。

经济权利通常是专有权。就实践而言，包括两层意思。首先应由权利所有人在其权利范围内授权他人从事这些活动。所以，任何人若想在作者的经济权利范围内使用被保护的作品（例如出版一本小说或录制一首歌曲），都必须获得权利所有人对此事的授权。权利所有人可决定使用的条件，包括报酬。

其次，作者也有权利不授权给可能的使用者（拒绝权）。在这种情况下，若使用者继续其行为（例如在被拒绝授权后仍公演某戏剧），作者可提起版权侵权之诉。

值得注意的是，经济权利并非总是一项专有性的权利。在某些情况下，国内立法和国际条约允许使用者不需或未得到权利人的授权而使用作品，但是，使用者要支付报酬以补偿被使用作品的作者。如果发生这种情况，作者权利就限于获得报酬权而不再

right owner, provided, however, that the user pays a remuneration in order to compensate the author for the use of the work. If and when such situations occur, authors' rights are limited to a right of remuneration, and are no longer of an exclusive nature. The public lending right and the resale right (*droit de suite*) are two examples of the so-called remuneration rights.

Economic rights are traditionally granted as a bundle of single prerogatives that correspond to the different ways in which a work may reach its audience. Each prerogative may be exercised separately. For instance, the dramatist who assigns to a publisher the right to publish his or her play in book format, does not thereby consent to the public performance of the play.

In compliance with several international conventions, most countries recognize today a certain standard catalogue of economic rights, which has constantly expanded with the evolution of ever more efficient means of reproduction and communication.

Economic Rights
• Exclusive rights and remuneration rights
• Usually a bundle of prerogatives corresponding to different uses
• Minimum standards guaranteed by international treaties

Most Important Economic Rights
• Right of Reproduction
• Right of Distribution
• Rental and Lending Rights
• Rights of Communication to the Public (incl. Right of Making Available)
• *Droit de suite* (Resale Right)
• Adaptation Right (incl. Translation)

是专有性的权利。公众借阅权和追续权（droit de suite）就是所谓获得报酬权的两个例子。

经济权利传统上是一组权利，以适应公众获得作品的不同方式。每项权利都可以单独行使。例如，戏剧家向出版商转让以出书的形式出版其戏剧的权利，但并不同意公开表演其戏剧。

为了与许多国际公约相一致，今天大多数国家都承认某些经济权利标准，并且这些标准随着复制和传播效率的日益提高而持续扩展演化。

经济权利
• 专有权和报酬权
• 通常是与不同使用相适应的一组权利
• 国际条约提供了最低限度保证

最重要的经济权利
• 复制权
• 发表权
• 出租出借权
• 向公众传播权（包括向公众提供权）
• 追续权（转卖权）
• 改编权（包括翻译权）

What is the reproduction right?

The author's prerogative to authorize or prohibit the making of copies of the work (right of reproduction) may be considered as the most fundamental economic right, as the control of copying is the legal basis for a wide range of subsequent commercial uses.

In conformity with international law, *reproduction* is to be interpreted widely, covering all possible ways of copying a work, either known or yet to be discovered. Conventional examples include the printing or photocopying of books or articles as well as the recording of music and films.

Recent progress in digital technology has brought a wide consensus, enshrined in international agreements, that the storage of a work in digital form in an electronic medium also constitutes reproduction in copyright terms, even though the result is not visible. A single exemption has been made with regard to those temporary or transient acts of reproduction (*e. g.* caching), the sole purpose of which is to enable a transmission in a network and which have no independent economic significance.

The Right of Reproduction
• Right to authorize the making of copies
• Covers all methods known or yet to be discovered
• Includes storage in digital form (except transient acts)

什么是复制权?

作者准许或禁止对其作品进行复制的权利（复制权）可被视为最基本的经济权利，因为对复制的控制是随后广泛的商业利用的法律基础。

按照国际法上的规定，复制应该广义解释，涵盖所有的复制方法，包括已知的方法和迄今未知的方法，常见的例子包括对书籍或文章的印刷或影印，以及对音乐和电影的录制。

数字技术近来的发展形成了广泛的一致意见，并被规定在国际协议中，即以数字形式将作品存储于电子媒体中也构成版权意义上的复制，即使其结果是看不见的。一些暂时或临时的复制行为（例如，缓存）因其惟一目的是在网络上传播并且无独立的经济意义，因而被认为是不属于复制的惟一例外。

复制权
• 准许复制的权利
• 涵盖所有已知和迄今未知的方法
• 包括以数字形式存储（临时行为除外）

How does the right of distribution work?

Distribution means the putting into circulation of tangible copies of a protected work. While some jurisdictions consider it a part of the reproduction right, recent international instruments, such as the WIPO Copyright Treaty of 1996, have explicitly recognized the distribution right as a separate prerogative, which can be exercised and transferred independently. The economic right of distribution must not be confused with the author's moral right to decide on the disclosure or the first publication of her work.

The distribution right is subject to an important limitation in favour of the free circulation of goods which is usually referred to as the principle of *exhaustion*: when a particular copy of the work has been distributed for the first time with the copyright owner's consent, the purchaser of that copy may dispose of it, for example by giving it away or even by reselling it, without seeking further permission from the author. It is up to national legislation to determine whether the effect of exhaustion will be limited to the national territory where the copy in question has entered the market, or to a larger area: trading blocks like the EU or NAFTA apply for instance a regional exhaustion. World-wide exhaustion is another possibility for which domestic laws may opt, as international instruments contain no restrictions in this regard.

The Right of Distribution
• Right to disseminate physical copies
• Subject to national, regional or world-wide exhaustion

发行权如何行使?

发行意味着将受保护作品的实体复制品投到流通中去。一些国家的法律把发行权视为复制权的一部分，但近年来的国际公约例如 1996 年世界知识产权组织的版权条约明确地将发行权认定为一项单独权利，可以独立行使或转让。发行这种经济权利绝不能与决定发表或首次出版其作品的精神权利相混淆。

发行权要从属于商品自由流通的一项重要限制，即通常被称为“用尽”的原则。当一件特定的复制件经版权所有人同意而首次销售后，该复制件的购买者就可以处置它，例如可以把它送给别人，甚至可以转卖而不必征得作者的进一步同意。至于用尽行为是限于复制品进入的市场的那个国家领域还是更大的区域范围，则依国内法律的规定：像欧盟或北美自由贸易区这样的贸易集团需要区域用尽。世界范围内的用尽是国内法可选择的另一个可能性，在这点上国际公约并无限制。

发行权
• 传播有形复制品的权利
• 服从于国内、区内或世界范围内的“用尽”原则

What purpose do rental and lending rights serve?

The rental and the lending of copies of a work are, in a way, similar to selling such copies: in copyright terms, both acts function as forms of distribution. However, we have seen that the first sale of a copy generally leads to exhaustion of the distribution right. The copyright owner therefore has no say on further uses of the work and may thus not benefit from activities that occur subsequently to the sale, such as the rental or borrowing of the work. Moreover, when copies are borrowed or rented instead of being purchased, this may result in a reduced sales volume and hence less revenues for the copyright owner. Also, borrowing or renting a copy may be just the first step that precedes its copying at home. Instead of buying a computer program or a CD, one could rent it out for a modicum amount of money, make a copy of it at home—an easy and inexpensive procedure—and thus avoid having to buy it.

In order to reduce the harm that copyright owners may endure from such practices, most countries have introduced rental rights, at least with respect to cinematographic works, sound recordings and computer programs, which are the areas where right owners have suffered the most from rental activities. Rental means making the original or a copy of the work available for borrowing on a commercial basis, *e. g.* in a video rental store. This right is of an exclusive nature and right owners have sometimes exercised it by refusing to authorise rental activities that were prejudicial to their economic interests (for example, this has been generally the case for rental of computer programs).

In some countries a lending right has also been introduced. Lending

什么是出租和出借权的服务目标?

对一部作品复制件的出租和出借在某种程度上与出售这些复制件相类似：就版权而言，两种行为功能都属发行。但是，我们已经了解到复制件的首次出售通常会导致发行权的用尽。因此，版权所有者就谈不上作品的进一步使用，从而也不能从销售后发生的行为诸如出租或出借作品中受益。此外，当复制品是出借或出租而不是购买时，会导致出售量下降进而致使版权拥有者的收入下降。同时，借入或租入复制品有可能是在家里进行复制的第一步。某人可以只花很少一点钱去租借计算机程序或 CD 而不是购买它们，然后在家里就可以轻松地制作复制品——一种容易而廉价的程序——还可以避免花钱购买。

为了减少版权所有者因此类做法而带来的损害，绝大多数国家都引入了出租权，至少在电影作品、录音和计算机程序这些版权人深受出租行为之害的领域。出租意味着在商业基础上，例如在一家音像出租商店里，将作品的原件或复制件用来出借。这项权利具有专有性，权利人在其经济利益受到损害时可通过拒绝授权出租行为来行使这项权利（例如，计算机程序出租就常常发生这种情况）。

某些国家还引入了出借权。出借是建立在非商业交易基础上

takes place on a non-commercial basis, for instance in public libraries. While rental rights are genuine exclusive rights, the lending right entitles the author only to an equitable remuneration and is usually exercised through a system of collective management of rights or through state subsidies.

Rental and Lending Rights
• Address successive uses by multiple users
• Rental: on a commercial basis
• Lending: on a non-commercial basis

What are the rights concerning communication to the public?

The notion of "communication to the public" comprises a wide range of activities aimed at rendering a work perceptible by larger audiences (an indefinite number of people). In line with international law, a traditional distinction is made between the public performance of a work and different forms of remote transmission.

The right of public performance refers to the presentation or performance of works outside of the family circle and an author's closest social acquaintances. The right does not only apply to live concerts, staging of theatre plays and projection of movies in the cinema. The background music we hear in bars and shops (either live or recorded) is a form of public performance as well. In fact, the rights regarding the latter uses are often referred to as "*small rights*" (in contrast to the "*grand rights*" of staging dramatical or musico-dramatical works, such as theatre plays and operas). The "small"

的，例如公共图书馆中的出借。出借权是真正的专有权，出借权授予作者有权得到公平的回报，并且通常通过集体管理体系或国家补贴形式来实现。

出租和出借权
• 多个使用者申请连续使用
• 出租：在商业基础上
• 出借：在非商业基础上

什么是向公众传播权？

向公众传播的观念包含了很广泛的行为，其目的是使作品能够为广大听众（不确定的人数）所了解和感知。依国际法，传统上一部作品的公开表演和不同形式的远程传播之间是有区别的。

公开表演权是指将作品在作者家人圈子和其最亲密的社交圈之外表演或演出。这项权利不仅限适用于现场音乐会、剧院舞台演出和在电影院里播放电影。我们在酒吧和商店里听到的背景音乐（无论现场还是录制的）也是公开表演。事实上，后者使用背景音乐的权利通常被称作“小权利”（与舞台戏剧或歌剧这类舞台戏剧作品的“大权利”相对应而言）。“小权利”在今天的

rights represent today a considerable source of revenues in the music business. These rights are usually managed by collecting societies, which collect payments and pass them on to copyright owners.

The rights concerning remote transmission of works have been constantly extended since the early days. Today, they cover equally the transmission by wireless means (radio, TV, satellite) and by wire (*e. g.* cable-cast), as well as—since recently—the making available of works on-line (see below).

It should be noted that each time a performance, a broadcast, or another transmission is being made available subsequently to an audience in a public space, i. e. outside of the family circle, a new act of communication to the public takes place (usually referred to as "secondary use"). This act also requires the copyright owner's consent. Several subsequent secondary uses may take place when, for instance, a concert (public performance) is broadcast on TV, which is turned on in a pub.

The Rights of Communication to the Public
• Right of public presentation and performance (incl. small rights)
• Broadcasting right
• Rights of remote transmission by other means

What is the right of making available to the public?

Today, in line with international law, most countries have undertaken to grant authors the exclusive right to authorise or prohibit the making available to the public of their works in such a way that members of the public may access them from a place and at a time

音乐产业界中代表着相当可观的财源。这些权利通常由集体组织管理，收取报酬，再把报酬分配给版权所有者。

关于远程传播作品的权利自从早期开始就一直持续扩展。今天，它们覆盖了无线传播方式（电台、电视、卫星）和有线方式（例电缆传播），近来作品也可以在线提供（参见下文）。

应当注意的是，任何一次演出、一次广播或其他传播随后都是提供给公众场所的观（听）众，也就是超出家庭范围之外。这样一项新的向公众转播行为就产生了（通常被称为“二次使用”）。这项二次使用行为也需要版权所有者的同意。随后还可能发生许多项二次使用，例如一场音乐会（公众表演）在小酒馆演出时又在电视上播放。

向公众传播的权利
• 公开演出和表演的权利
• 广播权
• 通过其他方式远程传播的权利

什么是向公众提供权？

今天，依国际法，绝大多数国家已经授予作者以专有权，使作者可以授权或禁止向公众提供其作品，而公众可以在其各自选择的地点和时间获得该项作品。如上所述，这项权利是作者向公

individually chosen by them. As outlined above, this prerogative is conceived as an element of the author's broader right of communication to the public.

The main example of "making available" is the offering of works on the Internet. Yet, the right of making available goes beyond the present state of technology and aims at covering all possible situations involving access to works at times and in places individually chosen by the public that may come into existence in the future.

The Right of Making Available
• Aims at access from a place and at a time individually chosen
• Technology—neutral and future—proof

What does the *droit de suite* or resale right stand for?

The resale right, which is commonly referred to as *droit de suite*, its name in French, has been adopted by an increasing number of countries in order to secure for the authors of graphic or plastic works (*e. g.* paintings and sculptures) a share in the resale of their works at public auctions and by galleries. The artist receives a certain percentage of the resale price from the auctioneer or art dealer, but has generally no possibility to prohibit the transaction as a whole. The resale right therefore constitutes a remuneration right rather than an exclusive right.

Unlike authors of literary or musical works, visual artist can capitalize on the traditional economic rights of reproduction and public communication only in exceptional cases. Often, especially at the

众传播权这种广泛权利的一项因素。

向公众提供的主要例子就是在互联网上提供作品。然而，向公众提供权已超越目前的技术状况，其目标是涵盖将来可能产生的公众可在自己选择的时间和地点获得作品的一切可能的情况。

向公众提供权
• 目标是在选择的地点和时间获得作品
• 技术的中立和未来的发展。

追续权或再售权代表什么?

再售权，通常用其法文术语追续权（droit de suite），已经被日益增多的国家所承认，目的在于确保图形或造型作者（例如绘画和雕刻）在公共拍卖会或者画廊里转手再售其作品时能获得一份收入。艺术家可以从拍卖者或艺术商的再售价格中获得一定比例的收入，但是通常不能从整体上禁止该项交易。因此，再售权只构成一项获得报酬的权利而非一项专有权。

与文学作品或音乐作品的作者不同，视觉作品艺术家只有在例外的情况下才能利用传统经济权利中的复制权和向公众传播权。通常，特别是在他们事业的初期，这些艺术家为了谋生而不

beginning of their career, they have to give their works away for little money in order to earn their living. The *droit de suite* therefore plays a compensatory role, as it allows the artist to participate in a later increase of the sold works' value.

The Resale Right (*Droit de suite*)
• Entitles visual artists to a share in the resale price of their works
• Remuneration right rather than exclusive right

What is the adaptation right?

Making an adaptation means modifying an existing work to produce a new work, usually referred to as a "derivative work". Examples include turning a novel into a screenplay or a theatre play, as well as altering the arrangement of a computer program or a database. A special case of adaptation is the making of a translation, which, in some legislations, is addressed to by a separate right. The adaptation right entitles the copyright owner to authorise or prohibit the creation and use of derivative works.

The simple building, to one degree or another, on the ideas of others does not, however, automatically constitute an infringement of copyright. Everyone is free to draw their inspiration from existing works, and so are, for instance, most detective stories, romance or western movies based on more or less the same patterns. In order to speak of an adaptation, the derivative work must incorporate a certain portion of the protected work in a certain form, which is not always easy to determine.

It is worth mentioning that the author of the adaptation has her

得不为了很少一点钱而转让他们的作品。从而追续权就起了补偿性的作用，它使这些艺术家可以分享以后被再次出卖的作品的增值部分。

再售权（追续权）
• 使视觉作品艺术家有权分享其作品再售价的一部分
• 是获得报酬权而非专有权

什么是改编权?

改编意味着修改一部现存作品从而诞生一部新作品。它通常被称为派生作品。例如将一部小说变成电视剧或舞台剧，也可以改编计算机程序或数据库的排列。一项特殊改编的事例是翻译，这在某些立法上被称为一项独立的权利。改编权使版权所有人能够授权或禁止对派生作品的创造和使用。

然而一座单体建筑物，在某些方面使用了其他建筑的创意，并不自动构成侵犯版权。每个人都可以自由地从现存作品中汲取灵感，例如，大部分侦探小说、浪漫故事或西方电影或多或少地建立在相同的模式上。谈到改编，派生作品必须将受保护作品中一定部分以特定形式融入其中，而这常常不是容易判断的事情。

值得注意的是，如果符合保护标准，改编作品的作者对派生

own copyright in the derivative work, if it meets the criteria for protection. In this case, the use of the derivative work by third parties will require the consent of both right-owners.

The Adaptation Right
• Exclusive right to produce "derivative works" (incl. translation)
• Adaptation distinct from free use of ideas as source of inspiration
• Author of adaptation has own copyright in the derivative work

作品也享有其专有版权。在这种情形下，第三方要使用派生作品则须征得两方权利所有人的同意。

改编权
• 产生“派生作品”的专有权（包括翻译）
• 改编不同于对作为灵感源泉的思想的自由使用
• 改编作者就其派生作品拥有自己的版权

Limitations to Copyright Protection

Copyright laws must take into consideration both the interests of authors and creators and the needs of society for access to knowledge and information and try to strike a fair balance between these interests. In order to reach this balance, copyright is subjected to two sorts of limitations.

On the one hand, there exists a limitation in respect of *duration*: works are protected only for a certain period of time. When the term expires, they fall into the public domain and may thus be used freely by anyone.

On the other hand, during the term of protection, the rights of authors to control the economic exploitation (use) of their works may be restricted by *exceptions and limitations* laid down by national laws: they allow for certain free uses, for purposes described by the legislators, which could be made, generally, *without a pecuniary compensation*. Permitted *free use* of works is sometimes confused with the so-called system of "*non-voluntary licences*". In some cases, national laws may, in accordance with the international standard, substitute certain exclusive rights of the authors with such a system: in practical terms, this means that right-owners cannot refuse to grant an authorization for the use of the work by third parties, but they retain the right to receive a *remuneration* and to negotiate its amount. Typical examples of non-voluntary licenses can be found in the field of broadcasting.

版权保护的限制

版权法必须考虑作者和创作人的利益以及社会获得知识和信息的需要，并试图在这些利益之间达到平衡。为了实现这一平衡，版权要具有两种类型的限制。

一方面，保护期限是有限制的：作品只在一定期限内受保护。一旦保护期满，它们就进入公共领域，可以被任何人自由使用。

另一方面，在保护期内，作者们对他们的经济利用（使用）权的控制要受国内法上的例外和限制的约束。法律允许为了立法者们所规定的目的而对作品进行某些自由使用，通常没有金钱补偿。作品允许自由使用有时与所谓的“非自愿的许可”会混为一谈。在一些情况下，国内法可能会按照国际法的标准，以下述体系来代替作者的某些专有权：实践上，权利人不能拒绝授权第三方对作品进行使用，但他们保留接受补偿并就补偿额进行谈判的权利。非自愿许可的典型例子可在广播领域中找到。

Limitations to Copyright Protection
• Protection expires after a limited time
• Exceptions for certain legitimate uses
• Non-voluntary licences

How long does copyright protection last?

Copyright is intended to secure to authors, during their lifetime, and to some extent to their heirs and successors, the exclusive enjoyment of the fruit of their creative labour. After a certain time following the death of an author, however, the public's interest in free access to intellectual works prevails, and therefore the copyright of the author, or at least her economic rights, expire. A work no longer protected by copyright is said to be in the public domain.

With the increase of life expectancy, duration of protection has been constantly extended. Recent international conventions provide for protection during the author's lifetime and a minimum of 50 years after her death. Many countries, notably the United States of America and the European Union Member States, have introduced a term of protection, which includes the author's lifetime and 70 years thereafter.

It is worth noting that in some countries the term of protection prescribed by the law applies equally to economic and moral rights, while in others the protection of moral rights lapses after the death of the author (as allowed by the Berne Convention), and in a third group of countries, mostly those belonging to the European Continental tradition, there is no time limit for the protection of moral rights: in this case we speak of perpetual moral rights ("*droit moral*

版权保护的限制
• 保护在规定期限后届满
• 某些合法使用的例外
• 非自愿许可

版权保护持续多长?

版权保证作者终生以及在某些方面其继承人对作者创造性劳动成果享有专有权。但是在作者去世满一定期间后，公众就可以自由获得智力作品成果，作者的版权至少是其经济权利就到期了。当一件作品不再受版权保护时，就称为进入了公共领域。

随着生命预期的延长，保护期也常常延长。近来的国际公约规定保护期是作者终生及其死后至少 50 年。许多国家，特别是美利坚合众国和欧盟成员国，已经规定保护期是作者终生及其死后 70 年。

值得指出，在一些国家里，法律规定的保护期对经济权利和精神权利都是一样的；而在另一些国家里，精神权利的保护在作者死后即终止（已被《伯尔尼公约》所允许）。在第三类国家中，绝大部分属于欧洲大陆传统国家，对精神权利的保护无时间限制：这种情形我们称之为永久性精神权利（droit moral perpetual）。作者去世后，禁止毁损性使用作品的权利由作者继承人或公共权力机构来行使。

perpétuel".) After the author's death, the right to prevent derogatory uses of the work is exercised by either the heirs or by a public authority.

Term of Protection
• According to international law: at least 50 years
• In some countries no time limit for moral rights

Are there general rules on exceptions to exclusive rights?

All copyright laws grant exceptions and limitations in favour of certain groups of users or the public at large. The legitimate interests recognized by domestic legislations and case law that would justify the existence of exceptions may be divided generally into four groups: promotion of freedom of expression, access to knowledge, the purposes of justice and the public, and finally private or personal use. Yet, it must not be overlooked that the notion of "*legitimate interest*" may vary significantly from one jurisdiction to another. Therefore, what may be allowed as an exception in one country, is not necessarily allowed in another.

The limitations laid down in national legislation and the form of each particular limitation are usually determined by the assessment of the need and desirability for society to use a work, in conformity with the country's national policy and traditions. The results of this assessment process vary considerably from one country to the next: while some countries (mainly those adhering to the European Continental tradition) have adopted a very restrictive set of limitations on copyright protection, others include in their legislation comparatively

保护期限
• 依国际法：至少50年
• 在一些国家里，对精神权利无时间限制

在专有权的例外上是否存在一般性规则？

所有的版权法为了某一部分使用者或广大公众都规定了例外和限制。论证例外的存在而在国内立法和案例法上承认的合法利益通常可分为四大类：促进表达自由，获取知识，为正义及公众的目的，最后是私人或个人使用。但是，绝不能忽略在各个司法管辖区合法利益的概念大不一样。所以，在一国被承认的例外，不一定在另一个国家也被承认。

国内立法规定的限制以及每种限制的形式都按照国家政策和传统决定于社会对使用作品的需要和期望的评估。不同国家的评估结果是大不一样的：当一些国家（主要是那些遵从欧洲大陆传统的国家）采取版权保护的相当严格的一套限制，另一些国家则立法上允许不经权利人同意而采取比较广泛的限制。美国的“合

extensive provisions allowing acts to take place without the prior authorisation of the rights owner. The open-ended "fair use" concept in the United States and the more restrictive "fair dealing" one in the UK, Canada or Australia, are examples of the latter approach. It may be worth noting here that the exceptions and limitations have not been harmonised at the international level and that all but one of the exceptions provided for by the Berne Convention, are optional, i. e. national legislators may decide whether to adopt them or leave them out.

Nonetheless, the so called "*three-step test*" has come to be regarded as the international yardstick for exceptions to exclusive rights.

Initially introduced by the Berne Convention as a set of criteria against which *any* exception to the right of *reproduction* is to be assessed, nowadays it has been picked up by the most recent international instruments (the TRIPs Agreement and the WIPO 1996 Treaties) and serves as a basis for assessment of *all* exceptions to *exclusive* authors' rights: i. e. limitations or exceptions to exclusive rights should be confined to 1) certain special cases 2) which do not conflict with a normal exploitation of the work and 3) do not unreasonably prejudice the legitimate interests of the right holder.

General Rules on Exceptions
• Basically four categories of legitimate interests
• Concept and rules vary from one country to another
• Strictly defined exceptions vs. wider concepts
• Three-step test

理使用”概念和英国、加拿大、澳大利亚的更严格一些的“合理对待”就是后一种类型国家的例子。我们要注意到，例外和限制在国际层次上并未协调好，《伯尔尼公约》除一项例外以外，对其他例外都规定是选择性的，也即国内立法可以采用，也可以不采用。

然而，所谓的“三步测试法”已成为专有权例外的国际标准。最初由《伯尔尼公约》规定的关于复制权例外的一套标准，已经被近来绝大多数国际条约所采用，（TRIPs 协定和 1996 年 WIPO 条约）并且作为作者专有权所有例外的评估基础，即专有性的例外和限制为：（1）一定特例；（2）不与作品的正常利用冲突；（3）不应不合理地损害权利持有人的合法利益。

例外的一般规则
• 四类基本的合法利益
• 各个国家的概念和规则不同
• 严格限制例外 VS 例外的广泛概念
• 三步测试

Which are the exceptions in favour of freedom of expression?

Freedom of expression concerns essentially the possibility to seek, gather and disseminate information. These activities form an essential prerequisite to the shaping of people's opinions and values in a democratic society. Recognized as a human right by the Universal Declaration of Human Rights, freedom of expression is the reason for a number of exceptions to copyright protection introduced in order to allow members of society who wish to use a work protected by copyright in order to convey their own message or who merely would like to use the information and ideas contained in such a work, to make certain uses without having to seek consent from the right-owner.

The right to quote works for the purposes of criticism and news reporting and the right of reproduction of a work for the purposes of parody are of particular importance among the limitations recognized in copyright law for the protection of the users' freedom of expression and for the promotion of the free flow of information. Actually, the right to quote is the only mandatory exception provided for by the Berne Convention, which allows quoting from already published works under the condition that this is compatible with fair practice and to the extent justified by the specific purpose. The Convention contains no specific indications concerning the permitted length of the quotation, but some national legislations lay down precise figures in this regard. Finally, as a rule, the name of the author and the source of the quoted work must be indicated in the quotation or reproduction, in an appropriate manner.

哪些是有利于支持表达自由的例外?

表达自由主要涉及搜索、聚集和传播信息的可能性。这些行为是形成民主社会人民的观点和价值观的一个重要的先决条件。这已被《世界人权宣言》视为一项人权。表达自由是构成版权保护的一系列例外的原因，这些例外的目的是允许那些希望使用受版权保护作品的社会成员来传播他们的自有信息或那些仅希望使用作品中信息和思想的社会成员不必获得权利所有人的同意而使用作品。

为批评和新闻报道而引用作品的权利和为了诙谐讽刺而对作品进行复制的权利在版权法所承认的限制中格外重要，这些限制是为了保护使用者自由表达或促进信息的自由流动。事实上，引用的权利是惟一由《伯尔尼公约》规定的强制性例外，它允许在符合公平实践及出于特定目的的条件下对已出版的作品进行引用。该公约对于引用篇幅长短没有特别规定，但某些国内立法则规定了这方面的精确数字。最后，作为一项规则，一定应以正当的方式将作者姓名和引用作品的出处在引用和复制中注明。

Freedom of expression
• Secured through free flow of information
• Of particular importance: right to quote

How can access to knowledge be secured?

Some limitations, recognised in favour of schools, universities, public libraries and similar institutions aim at encouraging dissemination of knowledge and information among the members of society at large. These limitations reflect the idea that society as a whole will gain greater benefit from allowing certain specific uses taking place without the right-owners' consent, under carefully prescribed conditions, than from rigorously respecting the control of the right-owners over their protected works.

Typically, these limitations cover acts such as reproduction for the purposes of preservation and replacement of lost or damaged copies of works (in the case of libraries), as well as reproduction of copies of protected works for teaching purposes. The "utilisation of works by way of illustration" (this is the formulation used in the Berne Convention), may include the use not only of printed material, but also of broadcasts or sound and audiovisual recordings. Usually, those limitations are only valid for institutions which are non-profit and publicly funded. National laws vary significantly as to the content and form of such limitations. Also, a number of domestic laws provide for the payment of a fair compensation to the right-owners for some of the above free uses.

Among the limitations in national legislation which aim at

表达自由
• 通过信息自由流动来保障表达自由
• 特别重要的是：引用权

如何保障获得被保护的知识？

某些限制，被认为有利于学校、大学、公共图书馆和类似机构，以便鼓励在广大社会成员之间传播知识和信息。这些限制反映了一种理念，即社会作为一个整体，在精心限制的条件下，不经权利人许可而进行某些特殊使用所获的利益较之严格尊重权利人控制其受保护作品所获的利益更为重要。

为了保存和替换那些已经遗失或毁损的作品而进行的复制（如图书馆），以及为了教学目的而复制受保护的作品，就是典型的范例。使用作品作为解说（这是《伯尔尼公约》的用语）可以不仅包括印制品的使用，还包括广播、录音和音像录制品的使用。通常，这些限制只适用于非营利机构和用公共资金建立的机构。各国国内法对于这些限制的内容和形式的规定都大不一样。也有一些国内法规定，对于某些自由使用要向权利人支付合理的补偿。

encouraging the dissemination of knowledge and information, many countries have in recent years started to adopt specific provisions in favour of handicapped persons.

Access to Knowledge
• Exceptions in favour of educational institutions
• Usually valid only for non-profit uses
• Specific clauses for the benefit of handicapped persons

How are justice and government served?

The requirements of justice, law enforcement and the functioning of government have been universally recognized by copyright laws. Usually official texts such as decisions of courts and administrative bodies are excluded from the scope of protection. Certain laws do not grant protection for speeches made during legal proceedings, parliamentary sessions or other public events. Finally, in most countries protected works may be presented in courts and other legal proceedings for purposes of evidence without the authorization of the right owner.

Justice and Government
• Official texts often excluded from protection
• Free use of protected material in courts

What exceptions are made for the benefit of private use?

A number of laws provide that a work may be reproduced by the

在各国立法中旨在鼓励知识和信息传播的限制近年来已为许多国家采用以向残疾人提供特别支持。

获得知识
• 有利于教育机构的例外
• 通常只对非营利使用有效
• 为残疾人利益的特殊条款

如何服务于法院和政府?

正义的需要、法律的实施和政府的职能普遍为版权法所承认。通常诸如法院判决和行政机构决议之类的官方文件是不包括在保护范围内的。某些法律对在法律诉讼程序中、议会会议中或其他公开场合中所作的演讲也不给予保护。最后，在大部分国家里，被保护的作品可以不经权利所有人授权而呈送法庭和其他法律程序以作为证据。

法院和政府
• 官方文件通常不予保护
• 被保护的材料在法庭上可自由使用

哪些例外是为了私人使用的利益而制定的?

许多国家法律规定使用者可以为了个人使用或为了范围有限

user for personal use or for a limited circle of family members and friends. To qualify for this exception, the copied work must, as a rule, have already been made public and there should be no profit purpose. In order to compensate right owners, private copying provisions are usually (but not always) accompanied by levy-based remuneration schemes: they aim to compensate, at least partially, the right-owners, whose rights may be prejudiced by private copying on a large scale through, for example, photocopying of printed works or home recording of films and music. Levies are usually imposed on the sale of reproduction equipment, such as photocopying machines or recording devices, as well as on blank sound or video carriers, and administered by collective management bodies, often on a mandatory basis.

With the emergence of digital technologies the reproduction of protected content is becoming increasingly easy and inexpensive. This has provoked rather vigorous debates on the issue of private copying in recent years.

Private Copying
• Permitted in a number of countries
• Usually framed by levy-based remuneration

Limitations in the digital environment

The digital environment, the ever more increasing use of works over digital networks and the use of technological protection measures (TPM) and digital rights management systems, with the purpose to prevent illegal copying of protected works, have provoked a heated

的家庭成员和朋友而复制作品。为此例外而复制作品，原则上作品必须已经公开出版并且是非为营利目的。为了补偿权利所有人，私人复制的规定通常（并非总是）伴有在征税基础上的补偿方案：方案的目的至少是部分地补偿权利所有人，其权利可能被大规模地私人复制所损害，例如，对印刷作品的影印复制或对电影和音乐的家庭录制。税收通常对复制设备诸如影印机或录制设备以及空白音像载体的销售而征收。通常由集体管理组织在强制性基础上来管理。

随着数字技术的出现，对受保护的作品内容进行复制越发容易且廉价。这已引发了近年来对私人复制问题的激烈讨论。

私人复制
• 在许多国家被允许
• 通常采用以征税为基础的补偿方案

数字环境下的限制

数字化环境下，在数字网络上使用的作品日益增多，保护措施以及旨在制止非法复制受保护作品的数字化权利管理体系的运用，这些引发了热烈的讨论，讨论这些措施是否会限制行使各国版权法所允许的合法自由使用，以及可能缓解这一类紧张的解决

discussion as to whether these measures limit or not the possibility of exercising legitimate *free uses* allowed by national copyright laws, as well as to the possible solutions that may reconcile these tensions. Case law varies from country to country and the debate is ongoing: there is no universally accepted solution and it is for the national lawmakers and courts to determine on a case-by-case basis whether the general criteria of the *three-step test* are met.

Limitations in the Digital Environment
• Right owners fear enhanced quality of digital copies
• TPM and application of limitations
• Application subject to domestic law and courts

措施。各国案例法也均有不同，并且争论还在继续：不存在普遍接受的解决方案，并且立法者和法院应在个案基础上决定是否符合三步测试法的一般性标准。

数字化环境下的限制
• 权利所有人惧怕提高数字化复制的标准
• 技术保护措施和限制的运用
• 国内立法和法院对限制的运用

Transfer of Rights: Assignment, Licensing and Succession

In order to bring their works to the market, authors usually rely on professional partners such as publishing houses, record companies, or film producers. To that end, they usually enter into contracts under which certain rights are transferred or licensed to the professional partner against payment of remuneration. In this case we speak of contractual transfer of rights or transfer *inter vivos* (during the author's life time).

Copyright may also be transferred after the author's death. This case is referred to as "transfer of rights *mortis causa*".

Transfer of Rights
• Contractual transfer *inter vivos* (during the author's lifetime)
• Transfer *mortis causa* (after the author's death)

What are the basic rules of a contractual transfer of rights?

The contractual transfer of rights only concerns the author's economic rights. Moral rights are, in principle, inalienable since they are deemed to attach directly to the author as such.

Further, it is important to keep in mind that the ownership of copyright in a work is distinct from the ownership of the physical object

权利转移：转让、许可和继承

为了使其作品进入市场，作者经常要依靠职业上的伙伴，诸如出版社、唱片公司或者电影制片人。为达此目的，他们通常要签订契约，在契约中要向职业上的伙伴转让或许可使用某些权利以取得报酬。在这种情况下，我们常称之为权利的契约转让或“活人之间”（inter vivos）的转让（在作者生存期间）。

版权在作者死亡后也可以转让。这种情况被称为“临终时（mortis causa）所作的权利转让”。

权利转移
• “活人之间”的契约转让（作者生存期间）
• “临终时所作的权利转让”（作者死亡后）

权利契约转让的基本规则是什么？

权利契约转让只涉及作者的经济权利。精神权利原则上是不能转让的，因为它被认为是直接隶属于作者的。

进一步而言，我们必须记住作品的版权所有和作品载体的物体所有（个人财产）是不同的。从而，一个人即使购买了一幅

or material into which the work may be embodied (personal property). Thus, a person who has bought a painting has not, generally, acquired any of the prerogatives pertaining to copyright, such as, for instance, the right to reproduce the painting on postcards or to include it in a catalogue. Should the owner of the painting wish to carry out any of these acts, he should seek the author's permission and enter into a transfer of rights agreement.

Basically, there are two ways of transferring rights: by *assignment* or by *licensing*. Whichever way the author will decide for the decision depends on a number of factors, including the nature of the work and the laws of the country in which the transfer should take place. These options will be examined more closely below.

Finally it is important to point out that economic rights are traditionally granted as a bundle of single prerogatives that correspond to the different ways in which a work may reach its audience. Each prerogative may be exercised and hence transferred or licensed separately. For instance, the author of a play who assigns to a publisher the right to publish her play in book format does not thereby consent to the public performance of the play. Similarly, the author of a novel written, say, in English, may assign or license to a publisher the right to publish and distribute her novel, she may also enter into agreements with other publishers who wish to publish a translation of the novel in a foreign language (unless she has already assigned or licensed the translation right to the initial publisher), and finally she may also sign a contract with a film producer for the adaptation right of the novel.

画，他通常也无法获得这幅画版权意义上的任何权利。例如，在明信片上复制这幅画的权利或者将其收入目录的权利。如果画的所有人想实施上述行为，他必须获得作者的许可并订立权利转让协议。

基本上有两种权利转移的方式：通过转让或通过许可。作者以任何一种方式作出决定都取决于一系列因素，包括作品性质和转让地的国家法律。这些选择将在下文中更深入地进行研究。

最后，必须指出，经济权利在传统上是以一束单项权利而授予的，以便能与观（听）众获得作品的不同方式相适应。每项权利都可以单独行使、转让或许可使用。例如，一部戏剧的作者向出版商转让其以书籍形式出版其戏剧，但并未同意对戏剧进行公演。同样，一部英文小说的作者可转让或许可出版商出版和发行其小说，她也可以与其他想出版小说外文译本的出版商签订协议（除非她将翻译权也转让给或许可给最初的出版商），并且她还可以与电影制片人订立合同，转让其小说改编权。

Contractual Transfer of Rights
• Concerns only economic rights; moral rights inalienable
• Transfer of rights independent of ownership of the physical material
• Two principal ways for rights transfer: assignment or licensing
• Each right may be transferred or licensed separately

What does a transfer of rights by assignment mean?

The legal consequence of the transfer of rights by way of assignment is that the assignee becomes the new owner of copyright and can take actions in her own name, including legal actions against third parties infringing the rights in the work. The assignment can concern copyright in its entirety or can be limited to one or more specific prerogatives.

Transfer of rights by assignment is typical for common law jurisdictions, which allow copyright as such to be assigned wholly or partially to third parties. The European Continental tradition, by contrast, considers copyright as exclusive incorporeal property since the work emanates from the personality of its creator. Accordingly, copyright laws based on that tradition generally do not allow rights to be assigned, be it totally or partially. In that case, licensing remains the only valid form of contractual transfer of rights.

Transfer of Rights by Assignment
• Assignee becomes owner of the rights
• Total or partial assignment possible
• Typical of common law tradition

权利的契约性转移
• 仅涉及经济权利；不能转让精神权利
• 权利转让独立于物之所有权
• 权利转移的两种基本方式：转让和许可
• 每项权利均可单独转让或许可

何谓通过转让方式转移权利？

通过转让方式转移权利的法律后果是受让人成为新的版权所有者，并且可以其自身名义行事，包括采取法律手段制止第三方对作品权利的侵害。转让可以涉及版权整体，也可以限于一项或多项特殊权利。

在普通法系国家中通过转让来转移权利是典型方式，它允许版权全部或部分转让给第三方。欧洲大陆传统则与之相反，因为版权来自创作者的人格，所以将其视为专有的无体财产。从而，建立在大陆法传统上的版权法一般不允许权利整体或部分被转让。在此情形下，许可是惟一进行权利转移的有效方式。

通过转让移转权利
• 受让人成为权利所有者
• 部分或全部转让
• 普通法传统的典型

How does licensing operate?

Unlike the transfer by way of assignment, the licence is an agreement whereby the copyright owner preserves ownership of the rights, but allows a third party to carry out certain acts covered by her economic rights, generally for a specific purpose and for a specific period of time. For example, the author of a novel may grant a license to a publisher to make and distribute printed copies, and, at the same time, she may license someone else to create a film script based on that novel.

A licence may be granted on an exclusive or a non-exclusive basis. A non-exclusive licence entitles the licensee simply to use the work in a defined manner concurrently with the copyright owner and, possibly, simultaneously with other licensees as well. A typical example is the licensing of the public performance right in non-dramatic musical works to bars, discotheques and similar public places, where music is played.

An exclusive licence means, by contrast, that the licensee may use the work for the purpose in question to the exclusion of any other persons, including the copyright owner himself. For the period for which it is granted, the exclusive licence has an effect comparable to a transfer of rights by assignment.

The Licensing of Rights
• Right owner maintains ownership
• Permission for a specific use
• Simple licences vs. exclusive licences

许可如何进行？

与转让方式不同，许可是一种版权所有人仍保有权利所有权，但许可第三方通常为特定目的在特定时期内实施权利人经济权利中的某些行为的协议。例如，一部小说的作者可授权出版商生产并发行小说的复制本，但同时她也可以许可其他人在小说基础上创作电影剧本。

一项许可可以是基于专有或非专有的基础上而被授予的。一项非专有许可仅仅使被许可人通常以版权所有人规定的方式与版权人或另外的被许可人同时使用作品。一个典型的例子是许可非戏剧性音乐作品在酒吧、迪厅和类似公开场合行使公开表演权。

一项专有许可则与此相反，它意味着被许可人可以排除任何人包括版权所有人在内而独自使用作品。在授权期间，独占许可的效力与转让权利相类似。

许可权
• 权利人保留所有权
• 允许进行特殊的使用
• 普通许可 VS 独占特许

Are there limitations for the contractual transfer of rights?

Transfers of rights are made contractually and therefore the principle of *contractual freedom* applies to such transfers. Yet many copyright laws, especially in countries following the European Continental tradition, lay down certain restrictions in order to protect the authors, who typically have less bargaining power than their business partners.

For instance, where partial transfers are concerned, many laws provide for a rather strict interpretation of contractual provisions, according to which the transferee acquires only such rights as specifically formulated in the contract. The rights that have not been transferred expressly will remain with the author. This means that when the author of a dramatic work transfers to a publisher the right to publish the work in book form, other prerogatives such as the right to authorize a stage performance of the play will not be affected.

Other limitations may concern the transfer of rights for types of uses which do not exist, or that could not have been foreseen, at the time the contract was signed. The underlying idea is to make sure that the author does not unconsciously give away assets which may later become a valuable source of income. An example would be the new digital uses of works (such as the dissemination of texts and other content via the Internet). A book publisher who had, for instance, acquired all rights to communicate a work to the public, but at a time where the exploitation of works through Internet did not exist, might have again had, in certain countries, to enter into negotiations with the author concerning the new uses. Last but not least, limitations

契约性权利转移存在限制吗？

权利转移由契约产生，从而契约自由原则也适用于这种情况。然而许多版权法，特别是遵循欧洲大陆传统的国家规定了一些限制以保护作者，因为作者讨价还价的能力低于其商业合作伙伴。

例如，当涉及部分权利转移时，法律对契约条款都规定相当严格的解释，依照这种解释，受让人只能取得合同中特别规定的权利。未被明确转让的权利则仍保留在作者手中。这意味着当一部戏剧作品的作者把以书籍形式出版其作品的权利转让给出版商时，其他的权利诸如授权舞台公演的权利将不受影响。

另外的限制可能涉及签约时尚不存在的或者尚不能预见的使用类型。潜在之意是确保作者不会无意识地放弃其财产，而这些财产以后会成为宝贵的收入来源。一个例子即新型的作品数字使用（诸如经由互联网传播文本或其他内容）。例如，一位书商已获得向公众传播作品的一切权利，但当时通过网络来开发作品的方式并不存在，则在某些国家可以与作者就这些新的使用方式重新谈判。最后但并非不重要的是，关于作者对未来作品的转让权也存在限制。

exist also with regard to the author's ability to transfer rights in future works.

Protective measures may finally aim at securing for the author a remuneration which is proportional to the revenue obtained by the exploitation of her work. Some laws aim at achieving this through reserving a certain minimum percentage of the revenues for the author, while others entitle the author to demand a revision of the agreed remuneration if it clearly proves to be out of proportion with the revenues derived in the course of the work's exploitation.

Limitations on Transfer of Rights
• Protection of the author as typically weaker party
• Rules concerning scope of transfer
• Rules concerning proportionate remuneration

Are there requirements concerning the form and the content of a contract for transfer of rights?

Although there is no internationally binding rule concerning the form in which contracts for the transfer of rights must be made, most national laws opt for the written form, both for assignment and licensing agreements, especially with regard to specific types of contracts (the publishing contract is the most typical example).

The contract typically covers the period of time for which rights are granted, an enumeration of the rights transferred, the territory on which the work may be used, the royalties to be paid, the responsibility of the parties and the procedure for settlement of possible disputes between them. In some cases, national laws contain legal presumptions which apply when the parties fail to include some

保护措施的最终目的是确保作者从开发其作品所得收入中获得成比例的报酬。某些法律企图通过规定作者获得最小比例的报酬来达到这一目的，而另一些法律则授权作者，如果所得报酬明显与开发所得收入不成比例，则作者可以要求修改报酬的协议。

权利转让的限制
• 将作者作为典型的弱者进行保护
• 关于权利转让范围的规则
• 按比例获得报酬的规则

权利转让契约在形式和内容方面有什么要求？

尽管对权利转让契约的形式尚无有约束力的国际规则，但是大多数国家国内法对转让协议和许可协议还是选择书面形式，尤其是某些特殊类型的契约（出版契约是最典型的例子）。

契约通常涵盖权利授予的期间、转让权利的种类、使用作品的地域、版税的支付、双方责任和争议解决程序。在某些情况下，当缔约各方在契约中未载入国内法认为对契约生效不可缺少的某些要素时，则应适用国内法上的相关规定。通常欧洲大陆法会包含权利授予期限的条款。这些条款只在缔约方对这一方面未

of the elements in the contract, which the respective national law may consider indispensable for its the validity. Typically, European Continental laws may contain provisions which determine the period for which the rights are granted. These provisions apply only if the parties have omitted to agree on this element. In other words, this type of legal presumption replaces, in some cases, the missing agreement between the parties.

Formal Requirements
• Usually written form of contract
• Legal presumptions in some cases

How are rights transferred after death?

The author's economic rights may be transferred after death by will or may pass by operation of law to her successors in-title. The successors exercise these rights during the term of protection in the same way as the author herself.

As regards moral rights, the rules vary from one country to another. In certain common law countries, moral rights, if granted, expire with the death of the author. In countries where moral rights may last beyond the death of the author, the transfer is secured by succession either by will or by operation of law. Yet, as a rule, successors are not entirely free in the exercise of the moral rights that they have inherited, as they are bound by the obligation to respect the particular wishes of the author or specific legal constraints.

Some laws provide that, in the absence of designated successors or heirs to the author, the protection of moral rights is assured by

达成协议时才适用。换言之，在某些情况下，当双方当事人在协议中没有规定时，则推定适用法律上规定的条款。

形式上的要求
• 契约通常要求书面形式
• 某些情况下推定适用法律上的规定

去世后如何转移权利？

作者在去世后可依其遗嘱或依法律规定将其经济权利转移给其继承人。继承人在保护期内可依作者本人生前同样的方式行使权利。

至于精神权利，各国之间差别很大。在某些普通法国家，作者死亡后精神权利即消灭。在那些精神权利在作者去世后仍存在的国家中，精神权利通过遗嘱继承或法定继承而转移，但是原则上，继承者对其继承的精神权利不能完全自由地行使，因为他们有义务尊重作者的特别意愿或法律上的特别限制。

某些法律规定在作者没有指定继承人的情况下，精神权利由

designated governmental bodies: this is common in countries where moral rights are perpetual.

Transfer of Rights After Death
• Economic rights: freely transferable
• Moral rights: several models in different countries

指定的政府机构来保护：这在规定精神权利无限期的国家中是很普遍的。

去世后的权利转移
● 经济权利：自由转移
● 精神权利：不同的国家有几种模式

Protection of Related (Neighbouring) Rights

Introduction

Related rights, also called "neighbouring rights", are commonly understood to designate the rights granted to protect persons who are involved in the dissemination of copyrighted works, other than the authors of works. On the international level, the term is used, in particular, with regard to the rights of performers, producers of phonograms and broadcasting organisations. These people or organizations bring creative, technical or organizational skill that are significant in the process of bringing a work to the public. It was thus considered that they deserve protection.

National laws may also include under this heading, for instance, the rights of publishers with regard to the typographical arrangement of their published editions, the protection of photographs and even database protection and design law. In line with a number of international treaties, most countries today have introduced related rights into their domestic legislation. In this chapter, the expression "related rights" or "neighbouring rights" will be used to designate only the rights that are devised for the protection of performers, phonogram producers and broadcasting organisations.

相关权利（邻接权）的保护

引言

相关权利，也被称为“邻接权”，通常是指保护版权作品传播者的权利，而不是保护作品作者的权利。在国际层面上，这一术语特别是指表演者、录音制品制造者和广播组织的权利。这些具有开创性、技术性和组织性技巧的人或组织在向公众传播作品的过程中是很重要的，因而他们应受保护。

一些国内法在邻接权这一标题下也包括诸如出版商在出版时的版式安排的权利、照片保护权，甚至于数据库保护权及设计法上的保护权。为了保持与许多国际条约一致，现今大多数国家已将相关权利引入其国内立法。在本章中，“相关权利”或“邻接权”这一术语仅指保护表演者、录音制品制造者和广播组织的权利。

Related Rights
• Protect the results of certain activities mainly related to the dissemination of works
The Most Important Related Rights
• Performers' rights
• Phonogram producers' rights
• Broadcasters' rights

How did the protection of related rights evolve?

Unlike copyright protection, where international law resulted from developments in national legislations, standards of protection of neighbouring rights were first discussed and adopted at the international level, before being gradually integrated into domestic laws. The first multilateral instrument on neighbouring rights was the Rome Convention for the Protection of Performers, Producers of Phonograms, and Broadcasting Organisations of 1961. The next major step was the inclusion of all three categories of related rights in the 1994 Trade-Related Intellectual Property Aspects (TRIPs) Agreement within the framework of the then newly founded World Trade Organisation (WTO). Finally, the 1996 WIPO Performances and Phonograms Treaty (WPPT) aimed to adjust the international protection of the rights of performers and producers of phonograms to the challenges of the digital age.

相关权利
• 保护主要与作品传播相关的一些行为的成果
最重要的相关权利
• 表演者权利
• 录音制品制作者权利
• 广播者权利

对相关权利的保护是如何发展起来的？

版权保护是先有国内立法而后发展形成国际法，相关权利的保护标准则是先在国际层面上讨论和接受，再渐渐纳入国内法。第一个关于相关权利的国际多边公约是 1961 年《保护表演者、录音制品制作者和广播组织罗马公约》。其后的重要步骤是新建立的世界贸易组织（WTO）的组成框架之一的《与贸易有关的知识产权协定》（TRIPs）（1994）。最后，是旨在调整应对数字时代对表演者权利和录音制作者权利的挑战而制订的 1996 年《世界知识产权组织（WIPO）表演和录音制品公约》。

The Development of International Related Rights Protection
• The Rome Convention of 1961
• The TRIPs Agreement of 1994
• The 1996 WIPO Performances and Phonograms Treaty

What are the characteristics of neighbouring or related rights?

The term neighbouring or related rights, established through usage, applies to a variety of persons. Each category is protected for different reasons. While, for instance, the performance bears the mark of the performer's personality in a way, comparable to the way the work reflects the personality of its author, the activities of producers of phonograms and broadcasting organisations are of a much more technical and organisational nature.

The expression "related" or "neighbouring" suggests a degree of closeness to copyright and at the same time distinguishes the rights in question from the latter. For example, in the case of a song, copyright belongs to the lyricist and to the composer. The performers of the song (singers, musicians), the producer who records the song on a CD, and the broadcaster who transmits a program containing this song, will have a neighbouring right, each one with respect to her contribution—i. e. the performance, the sound recording or the broadcast.

The terminology of related or neighbouring rights reflects the European Continental author's rights concept of copyright, where subject matter other than "works" in the strict sense is classified

国际相关权利保护的发展
•1961 年的《罗马公约》
•1994 年的 TRIPs 协定
•1996 年《WIPO 表演与录音制品公约》

邻接权或相关权利的特征是什么？

邻接权或相关权利这个术语是通过习惯建立而适用于不同类型的人。每一项权利均因不同原因而受保护。例如，与作品反映作者的人格相类似，表演则相应地带有表演者的人格标记；录音制品作者和广播组织的行为则更具有技术性和组织性。

“相关”或“邻接”这一表述显示在一定程度上与版权的紧密关系，但同时又与版权有所区别。例如，一首歌曲的版权属于词作者和曲作者。但歌曲的表演者（歌手、音乐家），录制歌曲的 CD 制造者和传播歌曲节目的广播者则享有邻接权，任何人都要尊重其所作出的贡献，即表演、录音和广播。

相关权利或邻接权这个术语反映了欧洲大陆作者权利的版权概念，邻接权的客体与严格意义上的“作品”是属于不同范畴

under separate categories of rights. In common law countries the producers of sound recordings and broadcasters traditionally have "copyright" in their productions and broadcasts.

Protection under related rights is similar to copyright, although the prerogatives granted to performers, producers of phonograms and broadcasting organisations are more limited in scope. Related rights, as a rule, are freely transferable and subject to comparable exceptions and limitations as authors' rights, according to the relevant international conventions.

The Characteristics of Related Rights
• Covering a variety of heterogeneous subject matter
• Terminology reflects personality-centred author's rights approach
• Protection similar to copyright though more limited

How are performers' rights protected?

The 1961 Rome Convention defines performers as actors, singers, musicians, dancers, conductors and other persons that perform literary or artistic works. Under this definition, "works" apply to the creations that qualify for copyright protection, irrespective of the fact that such a work may have already fallen into the public domain at the time of the performance. For example, under this definition, a performer of a work composed by Beethoven or Chopin would qualify for protection under the Rome Convention. The WPPT of 1996 has additionally introduced protection for the performance of "expressions of folklore", i. e. creations of local communities that have been developed through several generations and which are therefore normally

的权利。在普通法国家，录音的制作者和广播者在传统上对其产品和广播拥有“版权”。

相关权利的保护与版权类似，尽管授予表演者、录音制品制作者和广播组织的权利在范围上更窄一些。通常，相关权利可自由转让，并且依照有关国际公约，与作者权利一样有相当的例外和限制。

相关权利的特征
• 覆盖了众多不同性质的客体
• 这一术语反映了以作者人格为中心的权利
• 与版权保护类似，但范围更窄一些

表演者权利如何保护？

1961 年《罗马公约》将表演者定义为演员、歌唱家、音乐家、舞蹈家、指挥者及其他表演文学或艺术作品的人。在此定义下，“作品”适用于符合版权保护的创作，而不问表演时的该项作品是否已进入公有领域。例如，在此定义下，贝多芬或者肖邦创作的作品的表演者就合乎《罗马公约》的保护规定。1996 年的 WPPT 又引入了表演民间文学艺术表达的保护，即土著社会历经几代人发展的创作，而这些创作通常不符合版权法的保护。许多国内法已采纳了更为宽泛的定义，特别是包括各种杂耍和杂技艺术家。

not eligible for protection under copyright laws. Many national laws have adopted an even broader definition, also encompassing, in particular, the activities of variety and circus artists.

Along with the scope of application, the extent of performers' rights has also expanded since the early days. While under earlier treaties, performers were only accorded "the possibility of" *preventing* "certain acts", the WPPT has upgraded the economic rights of performers to fully-fledged exclusive rights. Performers have been accorded in particular the rights of reproduction and distribution, the rental right and the right of making available. In the case of collective performances involving a group of artists (like an orchestra), most countries concentrate the exercise of these rights in the hands of an elected representative.

Moreover, since a performer's activity is to some degrees of a personal nature, there is today a wide consensus that performers should also enjoy certain moral rights. Therefore, the WPPT provides them with the right to be identified as performers and the right to object to any distortion and other derogatory modifications of their performances.

Finally, the WPPT extends the minimum term of protection to 50 years from the date of the fixation of the performance or, if unfixed, from the date of the performance itself, whereas under the Rome Convention, the term of protection is 20 years.

Protection of Performers' Rights
• "Performer": usually one who performs works or expressions of folklore
• Rights of reproduction, distribution, rental and making available
• Moral rights of identification and integrity
• Minimum term of protection 50 years under the WPPT

随着适用范围的扩展，表演者权利的范围从早期以来也在不断扩展。在早期的条约下，表演者仅仅被授予禁止某些行为的“可能性”，而 WPPT 则将表演者经济权利上升为完整的专有权利。表演者特别被授予复制权、发行权、出租权和向公众提供权。在集体表演情况中，还涉及艺术家团体（如交响乐团），大多数国家将这些权利的行使集中到选举出的代表手中。

此外，因为表演者的行为在一定程度上具有个人属性，所以如今广泛一致认为表演者应该享有某些精神权利。于是，WPPT 授予表演者以身份权，以及反对对其表演的任何扭曲和其他毁损性修改的权利。

最后，WPPT 将最低保护期延长到从表演被固定之日起 50 年，若未固定，依《罗马公约》，保护期则从表演之日起 20 年。

表演者权利的保护
• 表演者：通常是表演作品或民间文学艺术表达的人
• 复制权、发行权、出租权和向公众提供权
• 确定身份与作品完整的精神权利
• 依 WPPT 最低保护期 50 年

What protection do the producers of phonograms enjoy?

In conventional law, the producer of phonograms is understood to be the natural person or legal entity on whose initiative and responsibility a fixation of a performance or other sounds is made for the first time. What is protected is the fixation of the sounds on a supporting medium, which is generally referred to as the "phonogram". The recorded sounds may, but need not be, works. Therefore, the recordings of bird songs or ocean waves, for instance, also qualify for protection.

Unlike performers, producers of phonograms have enjoyed, since the early days, an exclusive right of reproduction, to which the TRIPs Agreement has added the rental right. The WPPT, finally, has extended the protection, by introducing the new right of making available as well as the distribution right.. Like in the case of performers, the WPPT's 50-year minimum term of protection applies.

Protection of Phonogram Producers
• "Phonogram": Fixation of sounds of any kind on any medium
• Rights of reproduction, rental, distribution and making available
• Minimum term of protection: 50 years

How are broadcasters protected?

Under international law, the term "broadcast" is usually understood to involve the transmission of sound or images or both by wireless means. National laws may however interpret the term to also

录音制品制作者享有何种保护？

在条约法上，录音制品制作者是指首次将表演的声音或其他声音录制下来的自然人或法人。受保护的是录制声音的载体，通常被称为“录音制品”。被录制的声音可能是，但不一定是作品。所以，例如鸟鸣或海浪声音的录制也符合保护要求。

与表演者不同，录音制品制作者自早年就享有专有复制权，TRIPs 协定还增加了出租权。最后，WPPT 还扩展了保护，引入了新的向公众提供权和发行权。与表演者一样，WPPT 也规定了 50 年的最低保护期。

录音制品制作者的保护
• 录音制品：任何种类的声音在任何媒体上的录制
• 复制权、出租权、发行权和向公众提供权
• 最低保护期：50 年

如何保护广播者？

在国际法上，“广播”这一术语通常是指用无线方式传输声音或/和图像。但国内法也可能将这一术语解释为包括用电缆及其他类似技术方法的传输。广播者是那些可以对节目，包括节目

include transmission by cable and other similar technical means. A broadcaster is the natural person or legal entity that makes the decisions concerning the programming, including the day and time of the broadcast. The person or entity which merely provides for the technical equipment through which the signals are transmitted (e. g. network operators, etc.) is not considered to be a broadcaster. Broadcasts are protected as such, irrespective of whether they contain works in the strict copyright sense or other content.

Already the Rome Convention has provided broadcasters with the right to authorise or prohibit the re-broadcasting of their broadcasts, as well as their reproduction and communication to the public, the two latter rights being subject to certain conditions. These rights were reconfirmed by the TRIPs Agreement with slight modifications. The minimum term of protection under these two instruments is 20 years, counted from the end of the year in which the broadcast took place.

After the rights of performers and producers were updated by the 1996 WPPT, a discussion on updating the international protection of broadcasters' rights is currently taking place. While there is a general consensus among Member states that broadcasting organisations should be protected against illegal appropriation of their programme signals by third parties, some elements remain controversially debated, such as the inclusion of internet services ("web-casting"), as well as the concrete scope and duration of rights.

Protection of Broadcasters' Rights
• "Broadcast": transmission of any sound or images by wireless means
• Rights of re-broadcasting, reproduction and communication to the public
• Minimum term of protection 20 years
• Ongoing discussion on updating protection within WIPO

播出的日期和时间作出决定的自然人或法律实体。仅仅提供供发射信号用的技术设备的人或实体（例如网络经营者等）不能被认为是广播者。广播受保护与是否包含严格版权意义上的作品或其他内容无关。

《罗马公约》规定广播者有权去授权或禁止对其广播内容的再广播，以及对广播的复制和向公众传播，但后两项权利要遵守一定条件。这些权利在 TRIPs 协定中被再一次确认，但稍有改动。在这两个文件中，最短保护期是从广播播放之年年底起算 20 年。

1996 年 WPPT 条约对表演者和制作者的权利修订后，关于使广播者权利的国际保护现代化的讨论目前正在进行。成员国一致同意应保护广播组织以制止第三方对其节目信号的非法盗用，但有一些问题仍然存在争议并继续进行辩论，诸如因特网服务（网播），以及权利的具体范围和持续时间。

广播者权利保护
• 广播：通过无线方式传输任何声音或图像
• 转播权、复制权和向公众传播权
• 最低保护期限为 20 年
• 在 WIPO 中正在进行的保护现代化的讨论

Enforcement of Copyright and Related Rights

Introduction

As a general rule, any use of a protected work or other subject matter is lawful if proper authorization from the copyright owner has been obtained, except in certain cases prescribed by the law (see chapter on exceptions). Using a work or subject matter of related rights in a way that would have required authorization from its right-owner would constitute an act of copyright (or related rights) infringement.

Practically all legislations provide for a variety of civil remedies, penal or administrative sanctions when such acts of infringement take place. Moreover, in order to prevent infringement of rights from the outset, many countries have nowadays adopted additional legal provisions, in compliance with international copyright instruments, allowing right-owners to apply technical protection measures to their works. Among the important preventive measures laid down by many national laws are also the provisional and border measures, prescribed by the TRIPs Agreement "in order to permit effective action against any act of infringement"

版权和邻接权的实施

引言

除法律另有规定外，原则上，只要获得了版权所有人的适当授权，对受保护作品或其客体的使用都是合法的（参见有关例外章节）。使用本应由权利人授权的作品或相关权利的客体将构成侵犯版权（或相关权利）行为。

实际上，所有的立法都规定发生侵权行为时的民事救济、刑事和行政制裁。此外，为了从开始就预防侵权，如今许多国家都依照国际版权公约增订了立法措施，允许权利人对其作品采用技术保护措施。许多国家立法所采取的重要预防措施中包括临时措施和边境措施，这些都是由 TRIPs 协定所制定的，目的是允许对侵权行为采取有效措施。

Enforcement of Rights
• Civil Remedies
• Penal and Administrative Sanctions
• Technological Protection Measures
• Provisional and Border Measures

When does infringement of copyright and related rights take place?

Infringement may take place in the form of a violation of both the economic and the moral prerogatives of authors and other right owners. Economic rights are violated when a third party carries out one of the acts covered by them without the authorisation of the right-owner. Classic examples are the unauthorized copying of protected content such as CDs or DVDs, the illicit fixation of performances and the distribution of those products. The advances in digital reproduction technology as well as the emergence of so-called P2P networks have significantly contributed to a rampant increase in these activities.

By contrast, infringement of moral rights generally occurs in cases where the third party has acquired the rights to use a work but, in the course of utilisation, has acted in a way that is contrary to the moral rights. For instance, if the publisher of a book makes changes to a novel that have not been agreed upon, the integrity right has been infringed, and if in addition the publisher omits to indicate the author's name on the cover, then the right of attribution is violated.

Finally there are also cases in which both sets of rights are affected at the same time, the typical example is plagiarism. Plagiarism

权利的实施
• 民事救济
• 刑事和行政制裁
• 技术保护措施
• 临时措施和边境措施

对版权和相关权利何时发生侵权?

侵权可能是以侵犯作者或其他权利人的经济权利和精神权利的形式发生。当第三方未经权利所有人授权而实施经济权利行为之一时，经济权利即受到了侵害。典型例子如未经授权而复制受保护的内容如 CD、DVD 等以及非法录制、表演和发行这些作品。数字复制技术的进步及所谓 P2P 网络的出现对此类行为的急剧增长起到了推波助澜的作用。

与此相反，侵犯精神权利通常发生在第三方已获得使用作品的权利，但在使用过程中采取了有悖于精神权利的使用方式。例如，书籍出版商未经协议就改动了小说即侵害了作品完整权。如果出版商在封面上遗漏了作者姓名，则作品归属权即受到了侵害。

最后，还有两类权利同时受到侵犯的情况，典型例子就是剽窃。剽窃是盗用他人作品而归其所有。这至少构成了要求确认作

is the appropriation of the work of another and its passing off as one's own. This constitutes at least a violation of the author's moral right to claim authorship and her economic rights of reproduction and distribution.

Forms of Rights Infringement
• Infringement of Economic Rights
• Infringement of Moral Rights

Civil remedies

Copyright laws usually provide for two major civil law remedies: injunctive relief and award of damages. An injunction is the most effective way to immediately stop or prevent the infringing acts and therefore it is often the primary remedy sought in copyright infringement cases. Where an infringement has occurred or is likely to take place, the right-owner may typically demand for both preliminary and permanent orders. In order to secure discontinuation or prevention of the infringing acts, the court may additionally issue an order for seizure of the infringing objects, e. g. the unauthorized copies. Injunctive relief is available even where the defendant has acted in good faith, for instance, believing that the work or other protected subject matter in question had already fallen into the public domain.

The awarding of damages aims at placing the right owner in the same position as she would have had in financial terms, should there have been no infringement. In principle, it is up to the plaintiff to prove the actual amount of damages suffered as a result of the copyright infringement. However, since this might often turn out to

者身份的精神权利和经济权利中对复制和发行权的侵害。

侵权形式
• 经济权利的侵害
• 精神权利的侵害

民事救济

版权法通常提供两种主要民事法律救济：禁令救济和损害赔偿。禁令是立即阻止和预防侵权行为的最有效方式，也常常是版权侵权案中首先寻求的救济方式。当侵权已经发生或即将发生时，权利所有人典型的做法就是寻求初步的和永久的禁令。为了确保中止和预防侵权行为，法庭可能另外发布没收侵权物品，即未授权的复制品的命令。即使被告方是出于善意的行为，例如，相信争议的作品和其他受保护的客体已进入了公众领域时，权利人仍可申请禁令。

损害赔偿的目的是使权利人处于若无侵权、其财务状况本应具有的同样状况。原则上，通常由原告证明版权侵权所产生的实际损害数额。但是，这往往是很困难的，因而许多版权法允许在

be quite difficult, many copyright laws allow for a calculation of damages on the basis of a hypothetical reasonable remuneration, as a minimum amount. Moreover, in the case of moral rights infringement, many countries provide for additional monetary compensation of the plaintiff's moral damages. Unlike an injunctive relief, damages are usually available only when the infringing party has acted intentionally or at least negligently.

Civil Remedies
• Injunction and seizure of infringing objects (no bad faith required)
• Damages
• Monetary compensation for moral suffering (in some countries)

Penal sanctions

In addition to civil remedies, the infringement of copyright and related rights may also entail penal sanctions under criminal law. Depending on the nature of the infringement and the circumstances under which it has taken place, the sanctions may range from insignificant fines to prison sentences of up to several years. Usually, penal sanctions require intentional infringement and are generally applicable to cases where the unlawful use has been undertaken on a comparatively large scale and with commercial purposes (usually referred to as "piracy"). In compliance with their obligations under international agreements, in particular the 1994 TRIPs Agreement and the 1996 WIPO Treaties, many countries have significantly enhanced the possibilities to impose penal sanctions.

合理的假设报偿基础上计算出最低限度的损害额。此外，在精神权利侵权案件中，许多国家规定了对原告的精神损害提供另外的金钱补偿。与禁令救济不同，损害赔偿通常只有在侵权方的行为是故意或至少是疏忽时才可以提起。

民事救济
• 禁令和没收侵权物（不需要恶意）
• 损害
• 精神损害的金钱补偿（在某些国家）

刑事制裁

除了民事救济之外，对版权和相关权利的侵害也需要有刑法上的制裁。根据侵权的性质和侵权发生时的情况，制裁的幅度可以从数额不大的罚金直到数年之久的监禁。通常，刑事制裁需要有侵权故意并且通常适用于为商业目的的较大规模非法使用的案件（通常指“盗版”）。为了符合国际协议规定的义务，特别是1994 年 TRIPs 协定和 1996 年 WIPO 条约，许多国家都大大提高了处以刑事制裁的可能性。

Penal Sanctions
• Fines and imprisonment depending on the severity of the act
• Usually intentional infringement required
• Significantly enhanced due to compliance with international law

What role do technological protection measures (TPM) play in rights enforcement?

While digital technology has largely facilitated both legal and illegal access to protected works and thus increased the risk of piracy, it has at the same time considerably improved the enforceability of rights by offering right owners a variety of technological tools to control the use of their works: "Protection measures", such as encryption and copy control mechanisms, help to prevent the unauthorized reproduction and distribution of protected content, whereas "rights management information" allows to permanently identify the right owner or the terms and conditions of access to the work.

In compliance with the obligations arising from the 1996 WIPO Treaties, many countries have introduced a regime of legal protection, which prohibits the circumvention of those protection measures. The relevant provisions state that effective technological protection measures, including rights management information, may not be removed or otherwise circumvented. Additionally, the sale and use of devices or services that are primarily designed for enabling or facilitating the circumvention of such protection measures is declared illegal. Along with civil liability, the protection of TPM is usually backed up with penal and administrative sanctions.

刑事制裁
• 依行为的严重程度处以罚金和监禁
• 通常需要故意侵权
• 为符合国际法的规定而大大提高刑事制裁的适用

在权利实施中技术保护措施（TPM）扮演什么角色？

数字技术使合法或非法地获得受保护作品变得相当容易，从而也增加了盗版的风险，同时它也向权利所有人提供种种技术工具来控制对其作品的使用，从而显著提高了权利的可行使性。“保护措施”诸如电脑加密和复制控制装置，有助于防止对其受保护的内容的未经授权的复制和发行，而“权利管理信息”可以永久性地识别权利人或者获得作品的期间和条件。

为了与 1996 年 WIPO 条约规定的义务相符合，许多国家引入了法律保护的机制，以防止规避保护措施。有关规定确定了有效的技术保护措施，包括权利管理信息在内，不得删除或以其他方式来规避。此外，任何装置或服务，若其设计的主要目的是使能够或便利地规避保护措施，则这些装置或服务的销售和使用都属于非法。除民事责任外，技术保护措施通常也由刑事和行政制裁所保护。

It is worth noting that TPM are often contested by users and civil society who argue that they prevent certain lawfully permitted uses of the works, to which protection measures are applied. Case law on this subject is not unanimous and the issue continues to be in the focus of heated debates.

Technological Protection Measures
• Encryption tools and "Digital Rights Information"
• Legal protection against circumvention in compliance with international law

应该指出，使用者或民事团体常常争辩说技术保护措施会阻止合法性使用那些配备技术保护措施的作品。在这个问题上，案例法的处理是不一致的，这仍将是激烈争论的焦点。

技术保护措施
• 电脑加密工具和“数字权利信息”
• 依国际法，反规避的法律保护

Collective Management of Copyright and Related Rights

Introduction

Collective management of rights plays an important role in those cases where protected works are so widely used that it becomes difficult, if not impossible, to individually negotiate licences. The author may not be able to monitor all the uses at all times and in an indefinite number of places around the world. On the other hand users have no possibility to enter into worldwide negotiations with countless authors and other right-owners on a one-by-one basis. The performance of music in various broadcasts, as well as in restaurants, bars or shopping malls is only one of many examples.

The primary role of collective management organisation is therefore to act as an intermediary between right-owners, on the one hand, and users, on the other. It administers, usually as a trustee, the rights of its members and collects and distributes royalties on their behalf. However, according to the categories of rights, there are varying forms of collective management, which may sometimes include elements of individual licensing (this is the case, for example, of the collective management of rights in dramatic works). Apart from the administration of rights, collective management organisations may also carry out a variety of additional cultural and social activities.

版权和相关权利的集体管理

引言

权利的集体管理在有些情况下发挥重要作用，在受保护作品被广泛使用的情况下，单独授权即使不是毫无可能，也是极为困难的。作者不可能对全世界各地、在所有时间内对作品进行的所有使用加以监控。另一方面，使用者也不可能在一对一的基础上去和无数作者和其他权利所有人进行世界范围内的谈判。如音乐可以在众多电台播放，也可以在餐厅、酒吧或购物中心播放，这只是其中一例。

集体管理组织最初的作用是在权利所有人和使用者之间充当中介。它通常作为受托人为成员利益来管理成员权利，代表成员收取和分配版税。但是，依照权利的类型，集体管理的方式是不同的，有时还包括了个人许可的因素（这种情况例如对戏剧作品权利的集体管理）。除了对权利的管理，集体管理组织还从事各种各样的另外一些文化和社会活动。

Collective Management of Rights
• Takes place where individual licenses are impractical
• Collective bodies act on behalf of individual right owners
• Additional cultural and social activities

What are the origins of collective management?

The starting point of collective management may be seen in the foundation of the Bureau de Législation Dramatique (Dramatic Legislation Office) on the initiative of the famous French writer Beaumarchais in 1777. This body later became the Société des auteurs et compositeurs dramatiques (SACD). The first fully-fledged collective management organisation to be established was, however, the Société des Auteurs, Compositeurs et Editeurs de Musique (SACEM) —Society of Authors, Composers and Music Publishers, in 1851. This happened only shortly after the famous incident, in which the composers Parizot and Henrion together with the poet Bourget obtained an order against a Parisian *café-concert* for infringement of their rights by performing their works without a permission and without payment of a remuneration.

The French example was soon followed, first in Europe, then elsewhere. Today there exists an international network of collecting societies in more than 100 countries.

权利的集体管理
• 产生于个人许可难以办到的情况
• 集体管理的行为是代表个人权利所有者
• 另外的文化与社会行为

集体管理的起源是什么?

集体管理的起点被认为是基于 1777 年著名法国作家 Beaumarchais 创建的戏剧法律事务所。这一机构后来变成了戏剧作家和作曲家协会（Société des auteurs et compositeurs dramatiques，SACD）。然而建立的第一个完备的集体管理组织是作家、作曲家和音乐发行人协会（the Société des Auteurs，Compositeurs et Editeurs de Musique，SACEM）——1851 年更名为作家、作曲家和音乐出版人协会。作曲家 Parizot、Henrion 与诗人 Bourget 一起在巴黎人咖啡音乐厅未经许可也未支付报酬而演奏他们作品的侵权事件中得到了法院的支持。这一事件后不久，该协会就成立了。

法国的例子很快被效仿，首先在欧洲，然后在其他地方。今天在 100 多个国家中存在集体管理机构的国际网络。

The Origins of Collective Rights Management
• France of 18-19th Century: Beaumarchais and others
• 1777: Foundation of SACD
• 1851: Foundation of SACEM

What are the most important rights administered collectively?

Collective management primarily takes place in those fields where individual licensing would be too costly to be efficient.

The classic examples are the rights of composers and lyricists in the field of musical works, usually referred to as "*performing/small rights*". While at the time the first collecting societies were established, this category of rights included only performance of works in the presence of an audience, nowadays it includes practically all forms of communication to the public, including transmission via the Internet. The criteria for distinguishing between "*grand*" and "*small*" is the type of works involved. Grand rights concern, broadly speaking, the performance of all dramatico-musical creations, such as operas or ballets, while "small rights" refer to the non-dramatic forms of music. Only small rights are administered on a fully collective basis. The grand rights are, as a rule, licensed more or less individually, since the works in question are used far less frequently and their performance may be more easily monitored.

In hand with the performing rights in musical works go the so-called "mechanical rights", which concern the reproduction of works in the form of sound recordings (which need no longer be "mechanical"

权利集体管理的起源
• 18～19 世纪的法国；Beaumarchais 和其他人
• 1777 年建立戏剧作家与作曲家协会（SACD）
• 1851 年建立作家、作曲家与音乐发行人协会（SACEM）

受集体管理的最重要的权利有哪些？

集体管理主要发生在那些个人许可发挥作用而费用十分高昂的领域。

典型例子是作曲者和作词者在音乐作品领域中的权利，通常称为“表演权/小权利”。当第一个集体管理机构建立之时，其权利类型仅包括作品在观众面前的表演权，如今则实际上几乎包括了向公众传播的所有形式，包括通过因特网进行传播。划分“大”与“小”的标准是所涉作品的类型。广而言之，大权利涉及戏剧—音乐创作的表演，诸如戏剧或芭蕾舞，而“小”权利指非戏剧形式的音乐作品。只有小权利是在充分集体基础上进行管理的。“大”权利原则上或多或少是单独进行许可的，因为所涉及作品被使用的频率很低并且其表演也很容易被监控。

音乐作品表演权还伴有所谓的“机械表演权”，即涉及以录音形式复制作品（当然如今不再需要是“机械表演”了）。在许多国家，机械表演权与表演权由一个集体机构管理。

nowadays). In many countries mechanical and performing rights are administered by one collecting society. An important particularity of the management of mechanical rights is that standard contracts are negotiated on an international scale between associations representing respectively mechanical rights societies and phonogram producers.

Other important fields of application for collective management include the administration of rights related to more recent forms of commercial exploitation such as cable re-transmission and satellite transmission of broadcast programs, or to the collection of levy-based remuneration in countries which have introduced such systems in order to secure a fair compensation to the authors for the certain permitted free use of their works.

The Most Important Rights Administered Collectively
• Performing rights in non-dramatic musical works ("small rights")
• Rights of reproduction on sound recordings ("mechanical rights")
• Rights of satellite transmission and cable re-transmission
• Remuneration rights (e. g. reprographic reproduction)

In what forms does collective management exist?

The scope of functions performed by a collective administration body depends primarily on the category and nature of the rights it administers.

Collective management in the "traditional" sense applies in particular to the so-called "small rights". Under this system, right owners authorise one or more collecting societies to administer their rights on their behalf, on an exclusive basis, which means that the right owner, as a rule, may no longer individually negotiate terms

机械表演权管理的一个重要特征是，在国际范围内由代表不同机械表演权的社团和录音制品制作者之间谈判标准合同。

集体管理适用的另一个重要领域包括了对近来商业利用形式的权利管理，诸如对广播节目的电缆转播和卫星转播或对在征税基础上付酬的集体管理。某些国家已经引入了此种机制，以确保许可自由使用其作品的作者获得公平补偿。

集中管理的最重要权利
• 非戏剧音乐作品的表演权（小权利）
• 录音制品的复制权（机械表演权）
• 卫星传播和电缆转播的权利
• 报酬权利（复印复制）

集体管理以何种形式存在？

集体管理机构履行职责的范围主要取决于其管理的权利的类型和特性。

集体管理在“传统”意义上的适用特指所谓的“小权利”。在此体系下，权利所有人授权一个或几个集体机构在专有基础上代表权利人管理其权利，即原则上权利所有者不再单独对合同条款和条件进行谈判，而是由集体管理机构向未来可能的使用者提供许可，通常是以提供其音乐曲库中所有作品的使用权的空白许

and conditions. Instead, it is the societies which then offer licenses to prospective users, usually in the form of blanket licenses covering the use of all works in their repertoire. The royalties negotiated and collected by the collective body are distributed to the individual members according to rather complex schemes that aim to reflect the relative importance of the works and performances in question.

Yet in other fields, a collective management body may also operate more like an agency for the individual right owner who remains, to one degree or another, directly involved in setting the terms of use of the works in question. An example for the agency-type of collective management is of the area of dramatic and dramatico-musical works, where the collecting societies negotiate a general contract with organisations, representing theatres, for the exploitation of particular works. Yet, those agreements only specify minimum terms, while the particular performance of each play still requires the permission of the author in question in the form of an individually negotiated contract.

Finally, the so-called "one-stop-shops" are gaining increasing popularity. Under this concept, a coalition of independent collective management bodies offers licences that include several authorisations concerning different sets of rights. This centralised way of granting permission is particularly helpful with regard to audiovisual works, multi-media productions and all other works in which multiple right-owners may claim rights, such as the director, script writer, cameraman, etc.

可证的形式。版税也由集体机构来谈判和收取，再依照相当复杂的系统来分配给个人成员，以反映所涉及作品和表演的相对重要性。

然而在其他领域，集体管理机构的运作更像是个人权利所有者的代理人，在某种程度上直接确定使用作品的条款。一个代理人类型集体管理的例子是在戏剧和戏剧音乐作品的领域中，集体管理机构同代表剧院的相关组织就使用各个作品的总合同进行谈判。现在，这些协议仅具体规定了最起码的条款，而每一部戏剧的每次公演仍需要作者以单独谈判协议的形式予以许可。

最后，所谓的“一站式商店”正变得十分流行。在此概念下，各个独立的集体管理机构联合在一起，对于包括多项权利的几项授权给予许可。这种集中授权方式对音像制品、多媒体产品和其他多数权利人诸如导演、剧作者和摄影师的作品特别有帮助。

Forms of collective management		
Traditional	Agency-type	One-stop-shop
Collective bodies negotiate licences on behalf of individual right owner; No individual licences	Collective bodies negotiate general framework; Licences are granted individually	Coalition of collective bodies issues' licenses concerning a variety of rights of different right-owners in one work

How are collective management bodies organised?

The legal status of collective management bodies may vary widely from one country to the next. The forms in which collective management bodies is organised may also vary substantially, depending on the category of rights the organisation manages.

The first collective management organisations were non-profit-making private entities established by authors and sometimes publisher (often called "societies of authors" or "collecting societies"). Apart from this model, which is mainly European and South American, there are also private bodies other than societies of authors, e. g. BMI in the United States, which was originally founded by broadcasting organisations. Finally, in other parts of the world, especially in developing countries, collective management is carried out by public or semi-public entities on the basis of statutory law.

Apart from their legal status, collective management bodies may differ also with regard to the form and extent of government supervision, with regard to the number of categories of rights they administer, or, ultimately, with regard to the number of collective management organisations per category of rights. While in many civil law countries collective management bodies have in practice a monopoly

集体管理形式		
传统型	代理型	“一站”式商店型
集体机构代表单独权利所有人谈判许可；无单独许可	集体机构只谈总的框架协议；许可仍单独授予	集体机构联合起来对一部作品中不同权利人的各项权利授予许可

集体管理机构是如何组织的？

不同国家的集体管理机构的法律地位是大不一样的。集体管理机构的模式依照其管理的权利类型而有很大的差别。

第一批集体管理组织是由作者和出版商建立的非营利性私人实体（常称为“作者联合会或集体机构”）。除了这种主要在欧洲和南美洲存在的模式外，还存在私人机构而非作者联合会，例如美国的 BMI 最初就是由广播组织所建立的。最后，在世界的其他地方，尤其是在发展中国家，集体管理是由公共机构与公共实体在法律基础上运作的。

除了其法律地位以外，各个集体管理机构在政府监督的形式及范围上、在管理的权利类型数量上或最后在每一类权利的集体管理组织的数量上，也可能互不相同。在许多大陆法传统国家，集体管理机构在实践中就各项类型的权利都享有独占权，而在其他国家诸如巴西与美国的竞争法中，则不允许此类独占状态出现。

for the respective category of right, competition law rules in other countries, such as Brazil and the United States, do not allow such monopoly situations.

Differences also exist with regard to the way in which collective bodies obtain the right to act on behalf of individual right-owners. Usually authors and other right-owners become members of collective bodies by choice but some national laws provide a mandatory collective management for certain types of rights. A typical example for mandatory collective management is the cable retransmission right in EU countries.

Variety of Collective Rights Management
• Legal status: private vs. public bodies
• Number of organisations: monopoly vs. multitude
• Membership: optional vs. mandatory

How is collective management secured internationally?

The collective management organisation's scope of activity is traditionally confined to the country where it is set up, in accordance with the principle of territoriality. Most collective management bodies have, however, concluded reciprocal representation agreements with corresponding organisations in other countries representing the same categories of right-owners. Thus, a collecting society in any given country represents as a rule both national and foreign rights owners. Prospective users are therefore able to obtain licenses for practically the entire world repertoire from their national collecting society and at the same time, right-owners receive royalties for the use of their works

集体机构代表单独权利人获得行动权利的方式也各有不同。通常作者和其他权利所有人通过选择而成为集体机构成员，但某些国内法对特定类型权利的集体管理作了强制规定。一个强制集体管理的典型例子是欧盟各国的电缆转播权。

集体管理权利种类
• 法律地位：私人 VS 公共机构
• 组织的数量：垄断 VS 多样化
• 成员身份：选择性 VS 强制性

如何在国际上确保集体管理？

集体管理组织的活动范围传统上按照地域原则而限于其被创立的国家之内。但是，大多数集体管理机构都与外国代理同样类型权利人的同类组织订立有相互代理协议。因而，原则上，任何一个国家的集体管理机构既能代表本国权利人，也能代表外国权利人。因而，未来的使用者可从其国内集体管理机构处获得全世界曲库的使用许可，同时，权利所有人也可以从其作品的世界范围内的使用获得版税。

worldwide.

The cross-border cooperation between collective management bodies is to a great degree coordinated by international umbrella organisations. Among them are the *International Confederation of the Societies of Authors and Composers* (*CISAC*), the *Bureau International des Sociétés Gérant les Droits d'Enregistrement et de Reproduction Mécanique* (*BIEM*) and the *International Federation of Reproduction Rights Organisations* (*IFRRO*).

International Collective Rights Management
• Reciprocal representation agreements
• International umbrella organisations (e. g. CISAC, BIEM)

What are the advantages of collective rights management?

Collective rights management constitutes an efficient way to organise, on a worldwide scale, the lawful exploitation of works in those fields where individual licensing would prove impossible. Further, it is certainly cheaper to share the financial expenses of negotiation, supervision and collection of royalties among the greatest possible number of parties. As a result collective management enlarges significantly the choice of works available to the public.

By reducing the number of persons with whom users have to negotiate licensing contracts, collective rights management is, more particularly, beneficial in those fields where easy access to protected works is generally seen desirable, such as transmission of broadcasting programmes via satellite and cable-retransmission. With

集体管理机构之间的跨境合作在很大程度上受国际组织协调，其中有作者与作曲家国际联合会（*CISAC*）、录音和机械复制权管理协会国际局（*BIEM*）和复制权组织国际联盟（*IFRRO*）。

国际集体权利管理
• 相互代理协议
• 国际伞式组织（例如 CISAC、BIEM）

权利集体管理的优越性是什么？

权利集体管理是在世界范围内个人许可被证明是不可能的领域内组织合法使用作品的一种有效的方式。再者，它肯定会使为数众多的各方当事人用于谈判、监督和收取版税的经济开销大为降低。结果是集体管理显著扩大了公众选择获得作品的机会。

通过减少用户需要进行许可协议谈判的人数，特别有利于那些公众普遍愿意易于获得作品的领域，诸如通过卫星的广播节目传播和电缆转播。关于这些方面的使用，集体管理被认为是依某

regard to these uses, collective management may be considered as a viable alternative to a system of non-voluntary licences as allowed for under certain international conventions. Finally, collective management increases the bargaining power of authors. While an individual person is typically in a weaker position facing powerful corporate users, such as record companies, publishing houses or broadcasting organisations, uniting authors to a joint organisation allows them to be placed on an equal footing with their counterparts, thus providing them with a greater say as to royalty tariffs and other licensing conditions.

The Advantages of Collective Rights Management
• Facilitates licensing in case of individually uncontrollable uses
• Viable alternative to non-voluntary licenses
• Increases individual author's bargaining power

What challenges do recent technological developments pose to collective rights management?

The conditions of creation and exploitation of protected works have gone through significant changes with the progress of digital technologies, and this, no doubt, will also affect the future of collective rights management.

The advent of new digital technologies may, on the one hand, give rise to new forms of exercise of rights. It is argued that technological protection measures and digital rights management information devices will soon allow for licensing practices on an almost entirely individual basis through the Internet and by that eventually render collective management irrelevant. And even if it does not happen

些国际公约下所允许的非自愿许可制度的一种可行的选择。最后，集体管理增加了作者议价的力量。当个人明显作为弱势一方来面对强势的团体用户，如唱片公司、出版社或广播组织时，作者联合成为共同组织将使他们与相对方处于平等的地位上，也使他们在版税和其他许可条件上有更大的发言权。

集体管理权利的优越性
• 在个人无法控制使用情况下更便利于获得许可
• 对非自愿许可的一种可行的代替方式
• 增强了个人作者议价的力量

近期的技术发展对权利集体管理提出哪些挑战？

对受保护作品的创造和开发的条件已随着数字技术的进步发生了显著改变，并且这也无疑地影响到集体权利管理的未来。

新的数字技术的出现从一个方面而言为权利的实施提供了新形式。有人论证，技术保护措施和数字化权利管理信息将使许可行为很快就通过因特网几乎全部建立在个人基础上，从而最终导致集体管理无关紧要。即使在近期不会发生此种情形，但作者选择自由权的增大将对今天集体机构的准垄断地位产生影响并非是不可能的。另一方面，正在发展中的经济贸易全球化趋势使得建

in the near future, it is not unlikely that the authors' enhanced freedom of choice will affect the quasi-monopolistic position of today's collective bodies. On the other hand, the ongoing globalisation trends in economy and trade make the traditionally territorial basis for collective management seem increasingly inappropriate and discussion of supranational licensing schemes is taking places in different instances.

Partly in response to those and other challenges, new forms of collective management, such as the above mentioned one-stop-shops, have developed in recent years and there is a continuous tendency towards further integration among existing collective bodies. The survival and viability of collective management will greatly depend on its ability to prove efficient and attractive to authors and users alike.

Challenges for Collective Rights Management
• Digital technology may entail new forms of management
• Globalisation trends call into question traditional territorial basis

立在传统国家领土基础上的集体管理似乎越来越不合时宜，并且在不同场合也正在进行着超国家许可方案的讨论。

部分地为了回应这些或其他的挑战，新的集体管理形式，例如前面所提到的“一站式商店”形式，已经于近年发展起来并且有不断统一现存集体机构的趋势。能存活下来的集体管理机构将在很大程度上依赖于其能够证明对作者和使用人是有效率和有吸引力的。

对集体权利管理的挑战
• 数字技术可能需要新型管理
• 全球化趋势对传统领土基础提出的问题

International Copyright and Related Rights Protection

Introduction

Creations of the mind can be enjoyed anywhere at any time and are clearly not confined to a country's boundaries. Yet, every national copyright law has no effect outside its respective territory (the *rule of territoriality*).

In principle, every country is free to design its laws on copyright and related rights according to its own needs, policy objectives, and legal traditions. Particularly, it is in the discretion of domestic lawmakers whether and to what extent they want to protect works of foreign nationals. In the early days, culture-importing countries tended to grant little protection to foreign works in order to secure cheap copies for their interior markets.

However, with the growing importance of international trade relations, from the middle of the 19th century onwards, states increasingly started to conclude bilateral treaties for reciprocal protection of authors' rights. Today, a number of multilateral agreements provide a certain degree of harmonization of the protection of copyright and related rights in a wide range of countries.

国际版权和相关权利的保护

引言

创意在何时、何地都是有用的，明显不应被局限于一国国界内。然而，每个国家版权法在其各自领土之外是无效的（领土原则）。

原则上，每个国家均可依其自身需要、政策目标和法律传统来自由订立其版权与相关权利方面的法律。特别是各国立法者对是否给予外国人作品保护及给予何种程度的保护上是自行决定的。在早期，文化进口国倾向于给予外国作品很少保护，以确保其国内市场有低价的复制品。

但是，随着国际贸易关系的日益重要，从 19 世纪中叶以后，各国开始越来越多地订立双边条约来相互保护作者权利。今天，许多多边协议对为数众多的国家的版权和相关权利的保护进行了一定程度的协调。

International Protection of Copyright and Related Rights
• Rule of territoriality
• Harmonisation of national laws through international treaties
• Today, system of widely accepted multilateral conventions

The Most Important International Conventions
• The Berne Convention for the Protection of Literary and Artistic Works of 1886 (last revised in 1971)
• The Universal Copyright Convention of 1952 (last revised in 1971)
• The Rome Convention for the Protection of Performers, Producers of Phonograms, and Broadcasting Organisations of 1961
• The TRIPs Agreement of 1994
• The WIPO Copyright Treaty of 1996
• The WIPO Performances and Phonograms Treaty of 1996

What are the origins of today's international protection system?

In the early days, international protection of copyright was ensured on the basis of bilateral copyright agreements: that is, only two countries were involved. However, these agreements failed to provide a reliable legal basis for the cross-border trade with protected works as they were limited in scope and varied widely. Therefore, countries gradually turned to multilateral conventions which commit all parties to a single set of obligations.

The origins of today's multilateral structure can be found in a movement that evolved out of France about the middle of the 19th century, even before any bilateral copyright agreement was concluded. Authors and publishers called for a universal recognition of their rights.

版权和相关权利的国际保护
• 领土原则
• 通过国际条约协调各国法律
• 今天，有被广泛接受的多边条约
最重要的国际公约
• 1886 年《伯尔尼保护文学艺术作品公约》（最近修改于 1971 年）
• 1952 年《世界版权公约》（最近修改于 1971 年）
• 1961 年《保护表演者、录音制品制作者和广播组织罗马公约》
• 1994 年 TRIPs 协定
• 1996 年《WIPO 版权条约》
• 1996 年《WIPO 表演与录音制品条约》

当今国际保护体系的起源是什么？

在早期，国际版权保护是在双边版权协议的基础上确立的：只有两国涉及其中。但是，这些协议却未能对被保护作品的跨国交易提供可靠的法律基础，因其保护范围有限而且相互之间有很大差别。于是，各国逐渐转向能使所有缔约方承担一系列义务的多边公约。

今天的多边体系约源于 19 世纪、由法国发展起来的一场运动，当时甚至还没有订立双边版权协议。作者与出版商呼吁普遍承认他们的权利。1878 年由法国著名作家维克多·雨果在巴黎文学会议上发起建立的国际文学艺术协会（*ALAI*）的成立是具有

A decisive step was the setting up of the *Association Littéraire et Artistique Internationale* (*ALAI*) at the 1878 Literary Congress in Paris, under the sponsorship of the prominent French writer *Victor Hugo*. In 1882, the *ALAI* held a congress in Rome which addressed copyright protection at the international level.

Following the proposal of the German Publishers' Association (*Boersenverein der deutschen Buchh? ndler*), four meetings took place in Berne between 1883 and 1886 with the objective of elaborating a draft text for an international treaty. The Convention for the Protection of Literary and Artistic Works was adopted on September 9, 1886 and signed by ten countries—Belgium, France, Germany, Haiti, Italy, Liberia, Spain, Switzerland, Tunisia and the UK. Regularly revised and updated, the Berne Convention still remains today the cornerstone of international copyright protection, as most of the recent international instruments (such as the TRIPs Agreement and the 1996 WIPO Treaties) refer directly or indirectly to its provisions.

The Origins of Today's Multilateral Conventions
• 1878 Literary Congress in Paris, chaired by *Victor Hugo*
• Foundation of the *ALAI* and 1882 congress in Rome
• 1886: Berne Convention signed

How do international treaties afford protection of copyright and related rights?

International instruments do not usually constitute a directly applicable source of rights to private parties. An international treaty rather imposes obligations on the states parties to the convention, to

决定性的一步。1882 年，*ALAI* 在罗马召开会议，提出在国际层面上保护版权的问题。

依照德国出版商协会的建议，1883～1886 年期间，在伯尔尼召开了 4 次会议，目标是拟定一项国际条约草案。《保护文学艺术作品公约》于 1886 年 9 月 9 日被正式通过，并由 10 个国家签署——比利时、法国、德国、海地、意大利、利比里亚、西班牙、瑞士、突尼斯和英国。经过定期修改和更新，《伯尔尼公约》今天仍然保有国际版权保护基石的地位。近期绝大多数国际文件（如 TRIPs 协定和 1996 年 WIPO 条约）都直接或间接地引用其规定。

当今多边公约的起源
• 1878 年巴黎文学会议，由维克多·雨果主持
• 建立 *ALAI* 与 1882 年罗马大会
• 1886 年签署《伯尔尼公约》

国际条约是如何对版权和相关权利提供保护的?

国际文件通常不直接适用于私人权利。一部国际条约往往对其成员国规定必须遵守的义务，使其国内法符合条约的规定。在版权和相关权利领域，相关公约通过国民待遇原则和一些最低标

adapt their domestic legislation according to its provisions. In the field of copyright and related rights, the relevant conventions establish a certain level of protection in the contracting states through the principle of *national treatment* and the guaranteeing of a number of *minimum standards*.

According to the *national treatment* principle, works originating in a contracting state are protected in every other contracting state in the same manner as these states protect works originating in their own territory. For example, a textbook first published in *contracting State A* will be protected in *contracting State B* in the same manner as *State B* protects a school text originating in its own territory. The guaranteed *minimum standards* ensure that the protection provided by national laws of states parties—notably scope of rights, possible exceptions and limitations, as well as terms of protection—does not fall below the level agreed in the respective international instrument.

There are several possible ways for national legislations to implement international prescriptions. Therefore, in order to find out how copyright and related rights are protected abroad, one has always to consult the laws of the relevant country in which protection is sought.

International Treaties on Copyright and Related Rights
• Obligations on contracting states to adapt domestic laws
• Principle of *national treatment*
• Guaranteeing of *minimum standards*

How does the Berne Convention work?

After the adoption of the Berne Convention in 1886, several

准的保障在各缔约国建立了一定水平的保护。

依照国民待遇原则，起源于一个缔约国内的作品在其他任何缔约国均享有各缔约国给予本国作品的同等待遇。例如，一本教材，首先出版于缔约国 A，则它在缔约国 B 境内享有与缔约国 B 境内创作的教材同等的待遇。最低标准保障是确保各国法律规定的保护——特别是权利范围、可能的例外和限制以及保护期限——不低于各个有关国际文件所同意的标准。

各国国内立法有几种可能的方式来履行国际规定。所以，为查明版权和相关权利是否在国外受到保护，人们总是要查询寻求保护的相关国家的法律。

版权与邻接权方面的国际条约
• 缔约国有义务修订国内立法
• 国民待遇原则
• 最低标准保障

《伯尔尼公约》是如何发挥作用的？

1886 年《伯尔尼公约》生效后，历经了数次修改，最近一

revisions have taken place, the last in 1971 usually referred to as "the Paris Act". The signatory states to the Berne Convention are united in the *Union for the protection of the rights of authors over their literary and artistic works.* Since 1967, a specialized United Nations agency, the World Intellectual Property Organization (WIPO), serves as the Berne Union's International Office.

Along with the principle of national treatment and the guaranteeing of certain minimum standards, outlined above as basic features of the international copyright protection system, the Berne Convention enshrined internationally for the first time what is considered today as a common principle: the "enjoyment and the exercise" of copyright "shall not be subject to *any formality*". The convention leaves the question of whether copyright protection requires fixation of the work in tangible form to the discretion of national lawmakers. Similarly, the means of redress for safeguarding moral rights protection are subject to national legislation and therefore may also be found outside of copyright law, for instance under tort and contract law. The minimum term of protection includes the life of the author and fifty years thereafter. Contracting States are permitted to carve out exceptions to protection in certain cases, such as for educational and press purposes, and to substitute exclusive rights with equitable remuneration, in others. The only mandatory exemption concerns quotations from already published works.

Finally, the 1971 Paris Act introduced an Appendix containing specific provisions that allow for limited compulsory licences in developing countries, in order to facilitate knowledge transfer in those countries.

次是在1971年，通常称为《巴黎文本》。《伯尔尼公约》各签字国联合组成保护作者文学艺术作品权利同盟。1967年后，联合国的一个专门机构——世界知识产权组织（WIPO）履行伯尔尼联盟国际局的职责。

随着国民待遇原则和一系列最低标准的确立，国际版权保护体系的基本点也就勾勒出来了。《伯尔尼公约》第一次在国际上规定了今天被普遍承认的原则："享有和行使"版权不需履行任何手续。公约将版权保护是否需要将作品固定为一种有形形态的问题留给各国立法者去解决。与此类似，精神权利保护的救济方式也要依照国内立法。有可能是版权法之外的法律，例如侵权法和合同法。保护的最低期限是作者终生及其去世后50年。一些缔约国在某些情况下，如为了教育和新闻报道的目的可以规定保护的例外，另一些缔约国则规定可以用合理补偿来代替专有权利。惟一必须免除责任的是对已出版作品的引用。

最后，1971年《巴黎文本》还制订了一项附录，其中包含了允许发展中国家在有限的范围内实施强制许可的规定，以促进在这些国家内知识的传播。

The Berne Convention for the Protection of Literary and Artistic Works (1886)
• Several revisions, last revised in 1971 (Paris Act)
• Creation of the *Union for the protection of the rights of authors over their literary and artistic works*, administered by WIPO
• Referred to in later treaties (e. g. TRIPs and 1996 WIPO Treaties)
• Minimum standards concerning economic and moral rights, exceptions/limitations and terms of protection

What is the Universal Copyright Convention about?

The Universal Copyright Convention (UCC) was adopted at the 1952 Diplomatic Conference convened by UNESCO in Geneva. A revision took place in 1971 in Paris.

In line with endeavours that go back to the time of the League of Nations, the central objective of the UCC was to secure multilateral copyright relations between the countries of the Berne Union and those countries outside of it, which found the Berne Convention's standards incompatible with their standards of development or their own legal traditions: among the most important reasons was the lack of recognition of moral rights, the generally shorter term of protection provided for by their national laws and the existence of formalities as a condition for protection, such as registration of works.

The Universal Copyright Convention of 1952 provided a solution to these problems. It prescribed that the formalities required by the national law of a contracting state shall be considered to be satisfied if all the copies of a work originating in another contracting state carry the symbol (c) accompanied by the name of the copyright owner and the year of the first publication. It set a minimum duration for copyright

《伯尔尼保护文学艺术作品公约》（1886）
• 数次修订，最近一次是在 1971 年（《巴黎文本》）
• 建立了保护作者文学艺术作品权利同盟，由 WIPO 管理
• 有关的后来几个条约（TRIPs 协定和 1996 年 WIPO 条约）
• 经济权利和精神权利的最低标准，保护的例外/限制和保护期限

关于《世界版权公约》

《世界版权公约》（UCC）于 1952 年联合国教科文组织日内瓦外交会议上正式通过。1971 年在巴黎修订。

与回到国际联盟时代的努力相一致，UCC 的中心目的是保护《伯尔尼公约》缔约国与公约之外的国家间的多边版权关系。因为公约外的国家发现《伯尔尼公约》的标准与其本国发展标准或其自身法律传统不相容：其中最重要的原因是不承认精神权利，其国内立法规定的保护期通常较短，并且将完成一定的手续，如作品的登记、作为保护的条件。

1952 年《世界版权公约》为这些问题提供了解决办法。它规定凡在其他缔约国首次出版的作品复制件上标有符号（c），且载有版权所有人姓名和首版年份的，即可认为该作品符合该缔约国国内法关于手续的要求。公约规定最低版权保护期为自出版之日起 25 年，最具典型性的是不少于作者死后 25 年。最后，公约没有规定保护精神权利的问题。公约还特别规定了发展中国家

protection as 25 years from the date of publication, and typically not less than 25 years after the death of the author. Finally, it left the protection of moral rights outside the scope of the Convention. It also specified particular exceptions which may be applied to developing countries. Its norms are expressed in the form of general principles which can be given different shades of interpretation depending on the specific identity and national policy of each contracting state.

As the renowned French lawyer Andre Kerever has stated, the UCC "created a legal structure which could accommodate the United States, the USSR, the industrially developed countries and the developing countries". It also influenced its predecessor, the Berne Convention. Fruitful cooperation led to the closer alignment of the two Conventions, which were revised in 1971. This revision gave concrete form to the twofold movement initiated in 1952 by the UCC: "furtherance of the legal rights of creators and acknowledgement of the specific needs of developing countries."

The Universal Copyright Convention (1952)
• Revised in 1971 (Paris Act)
• Intended to serve as a "bridge" toward the *Berne Union*

What provisions does the Rome Convention contain?

The question concerning the international protection of neighbouring rights was first formally addressed at the 1928 Rome Conference to revise the Berne Convention. In 1949, three international organisations—the BIRPI (the predecessor of WIPO), UNESCO, and

可以适用的例外。其规范表现为一般原则的形式，可以依照各缔约国自身特点和国内政策来给以不同的解释。

正如享有盛誉的法国律师 Andre Kerever 所称，UCC 创建了一个能容纳美国、苏联、发达的工业国和发展中国家的法律结构。它还影响了在先的《伯尔尼公约》。富有成效的合作带来了两个条约更紧密的合作，两公约都于 1971 年进行了修订。这次修订使得由 UCC 于 1952 年倡议的两个方面的发展取得了具体的形式。发展了创造者的法律权利，并且确认了发展中国家的特殊需求。

《世界版权公约》（1952）
• 1971 年修订（巴黎文本）
• 意图成为通向伯尔尼同盟的“桥梁”

《罗马公约》包含什么规定？

关于邻接权的国际保护问题于 1928 年修订《伯尔尼公约》的罗马会议上首次正式提出。1949 年，三个国际组织——保护知识产权联合国际局（BIRPI，WIPO 的前身）、联合国教科文组织 UNESCO 和国际劳工组织（ILO）启动了这项工作。它们的集

the International Labour Organisation (ILO), took up this topic. Their joint efforts led to the adoption of the International Convention for the Protection of Performers, Producers of Phonograms and Broadcasting Organisations at the Diplomatic Conference in Rome in 1961 (usually referred to as the "Rome Convention"). The treaty was signed by 40 states and came into force in 1964.

The Rome Convention relates to the protection of performing artists ("performers"), record producers ("producers of phonograms"), and broadcasting organisations. It provides for a constrained version of national treatment which only applies with regard to the rights specifically granted in the treaty. While the producers and broadcasters are granted exclusive rights concerning reproduction, distribution and communication to the public modelled on authors' rights, performers have only "the possibility of preventing" various specified acts. This distinction was intended to allow certain countries, mainly of the common law tradition, to continue to protect performers on a different legal basis. The Convention guarantees a general minimum term of protection of 20 years, counted from the end of the year when respectively the performance, fixation or broadcast took place. Member states are allowed to establish certain exceptions for purposes such as private use or news reporting.

The Rome Convention for the Protection of Performers, Producers of Phonograms, and Broadcasting Organisations (1961)
• Jointly administered by WIPO, UNESCO and ILO
• First international instrument to address neighbouring rights

体努力使保护《表演者、录音制品制作者和广播组织的国际公约》(通常称为《罗马公约》)于1961年罗马外交会议上得以通过。条约由40国签署并于1964年生效。

《罗马公约》涉及对表演艺术家(表演者)、录音制作者和广播组织的保护。公约规定,只有条约中特别规定的权利才能适用国民待遇。制作者和广播者享有以作者权为范本的复制、发行和向公众传播的专有权利,而表演者则只对各种特定行为享有"可能制止"的权利。这一区分是想允许某些国家,主要是具有普通法传统的国家,在不同的法律基础上继续保护表演者。公约规定从表演、录制或广播之年年终起20年的最低保护期。成员国也可以为私人使用和新闻报道等而规定某些例外。

《保护表演者、录音制品制作者和广播组织罗马公约》(1961)

- 由 WIPO、UNESCO 和 ILO 集体管理
- 涉及邻接权的第一个国际文件

What has the TRIPs Agreement brought about?

The Agreement on Trade-Related Aspects of Intellectual Property Rights (TRIPs) was signed at Marrakech, Morocco, on 15 April 1994. As a result of the Uruguay round of multilateral trade negotiations, it forms part of the legal obligations of the World Trade Organisation (WTO), which is the successor of the General Agreement on Tariffs and Trade (GATT) of 1947.

The TRIPs Agreement thus links intellectual property protection to trade issues, in particular by making available the WTO's dispute settlement process, which can impose trade sanctions on members violating the agreement.

With regard to copyright, the TRIPs Agreement requires from WTO members to comply with the substantive provisions (with the exception of moral rights obligations) of the Berne Convention, which it complemented in several respects. More particularly, the TRIPs Agreement extended protection to computer programs and compilations of data and introduced an exclusive right to authorize or prohibit the commercial rental of computer programmes and cinematographic works.

In the sphere of neighbouring rights, the TRIPs Agreement set up its own provisions on the rights of performers, producers of phonograms (sound recordings), and broadcasters. Compared to the Rome Convention, it brought about an exclusive rental right for performing artists and phonogram producers under certain conditions, as well as a minimum term of protection of 50 years for these two groups of right owners.

In addition, the TRIPs Agreement extended he application of the so-called "*three-step test*" (i. e. the Berne Convention criteria for

TRIPs 协定带来了什么?

《与贸易有关的知识产权协定》（TRIPs 协定）于 1994 年 4 月 15 日签署于摩洛哥马拉喀什。作为多边贸易谈判乌拉圭回合的成果之一，TRIPs 协定构成了世界贸易组织（WTO，其前身为 1947 年关税与贸易总协定）的法律义务的一部分。

TRIPs 协定将知识产权保护同贸易问题联系起来，特别是通过 WTO 争端解决程序可对违反协定的成员进行贸易制裁。

在版权方面，TRIPs 协定要求 WTO 成员方遵守《伯尔尼公约》规定的实质性条款（精神权利除外)，但在某些方面则作出了补充。尤为特殊的是，TRIPs 协定还将保护扩展到计算机程序和数据汇编方面，并规定了一项授权或禁止计算机程序和电影作品的商业出租的专有权。

在邻接权领域内，TRIPs 协定规定了其自身的关于表演者、录音制品的制作者和广播者的权利。与《罗马公约》相比，它规定了在一定条件下表演艺术家和录音制品制作者的专有出租权，其最低保护期也为 50 年。

此外，TRIPs 协定将所谓“三步测试法”（《伯尔尼公约》许可复制权例外的标准）的运用扩展至所有的经济权利。这样

allowing exceptions to the right of reproduction) to all economic rights. Thus it established an additional safeguard in order to calibrate the limitations that contracting countries may impose on exclusive rights.

In order to "permit effective action against any act of infringement of intellectual property", the TRIPs Agreement requires that Member States provide for specified enforcement procedures including "remedies which constitute a deterrent to future infringement". Civil and penal remedies, as well as border measures should be provided for by Member States.

The Agreement on Trade-Related Aspects of Intellectual Property Rights (1994)
• Links Intellectual Property with trade issues within the World Trade Organisation
• "Berne / Rome *plus*" standard of protection (without moral rights)
• Specific obligations on states to introduce effective enforcement procedures

What is the role of the 1996 WIPO treaties?

On 20 December 1996, representatives of approximately 120 countries adopted the WIPO Copyright Treaty (WCT) together with the WIPO Performances and Phonograms Treaty (WPPT) at a Diplomatic Conference on Certain Copyright and Neighbouring Rights. The treaties were designed to address questions related to the impact of the new digital technologies on copyright and related rights. The WCT and the WPPT incorporate and update all achievements of Berne, Rome, and the TRIPs Agreement.

The WCT obliges the contracting states to comply with the substantial provisions of the Paris Act of the Berne Convention. Like the TRIPs Agreement, protection is extended to computer programs and databases. Along with a qualified commercial rental right, the

TRIPs 协定就建立了额外的保障以协调各缔约方可能对专有权所加的限制。

为了“准许对侵犯知识产权行为采取有效行动”，TRIPs 协定要求各缔约方规定特殊执行程序，包括“将会构成对未来侵权的救济”。除民事及刑事的制裁外，缔约方也应规定边境措施。

《与贸易有关的知识产权协定》（1994）
• 在世界贸易组织内将知识产权与贸易问题相联系
• “伯尔尼/罗马附加”保护标准（无精神权利）
• 缔约方有实施有效执行程序的特定义务

1996 年世界知识产权组织条约的作用是什么？

1996 年 12 月 20 日，在关于某些版权与邻接权的外交会议上，大约 120 个国家的代表通过了《WIPO 版权条约》和《WIPO 表演和录音制品条约》。两个条约的订立是为了解决在版权和邻接权方面受新型数字技术影响而产生的有关问题。WCT 和 WPPT 统合并更新了《伯尔尼公约》、《罗马公约》和 TRIPs 协定的所有成就。

WCT 规定缔约方必须遵守《伯尔尼公约》（《巴黎文本》）的实体规定。与 TRIPs 协定相同，WCT 的保护也扩展至计算机程序和数据库。除商业出租权外，WCT 规定了新的“向公众提供权”，其中包括个人在其选择的时间和地点通过点击，例如经

WCT introduces a new "right of making available to the public" which encompasses interactive transmission of works on demand, for instance via the Internet.

The WPPT draws on elements of the Rome Convention by spelling out minimum standards for the protection of performers and record producers ("producers of phonograms"), but also introduces significant improvements, in particular for performers. Apart from acquiring exclusive economic rights instead of the mere possibility to prevent unauthorized uses, performers are also afforded rights of attribution and integrity. This was the first time that moral rights were recognized to performers in an international agreement. Moreover, a qualified rental right, as well as the new "right of making available to the public" have been introduced for both performers and record producers. In comparison to the Rome Convention, the minimum term of protection has been extended to 50 years.

Both WIPO Treaties incorporate the "*three-step-test*" as established by the TRIPs Agreement and oblige parties to provide for effective remedies to enforce the rights under the Treaties. A key element in this context is the obligation to prevent the circumvention of encryption technologies and the interference with electronic rights management information, which is a new feature in the field of international protection of copyright and related rights.

The WIPO Copyright Treaty The WIPO Performances and Phonograms Treaty (1996)
• Designed to address new technologies and means of communication
• Introduction of new "right of making available to the public"
• Obligation to prohibit circumvention of technical protection measures
• Moral rights for performers

由因特网而相互传送作品。

WPPT 吸收了《罗马公约》的内容，具体规定了表演者和录音制作者（“录音制品制作者”）的最低保护标准，但也增加了一些重要的改进，尤其是在表演者方面。除了获得专有的权利以取代仅仅制止未经授权的使用的可能性外，表演者还被赋予归属权和完整权。这也是表演者的精神权利首次在国际协议中得到承认。此外，符合条件的出租权，以及新的“向公众提供权”也被规定为表演者与录音制作者的权利。与《罗马公约》相比较，最低保护期限延展到了 50 年。

两个 WIPO 条约也将 TRIPs 协定所建立的“三步测试”包括在其中，并使缔约方负有规定有效救济以执行条约权利的义务。在这一方面一个关键要素是负有制止规避加密技术和干扰电子权利管理信息的义务，这是版权和相关权利国际保护领域的一个新特点。

WIPO 版权条约 《WIPO 表演和录音制品条约》(1996)
• 制定两条约是为适应传播新技术和新方法
• 引进了新型的“向公众提供权”
• 有义务制止规避技术保护措施
• 表演者的精神权利